The M.G. MIDGET
(Series TF and TF 1500)
OPERATION MANUAL

AF271780

SECOND EDITION

A copy of this Operation Manual is sent out with every M.G. Midget (Series TF and TF 1500) car. Additional copies are obtainable only from your M.G. Distributor and Part No. AKD658A should be quoted when ordering.

ENGINE AND CHASSIS NUMBERS

The engine and chassis numbers of M.G. Midget cars are located on a plate mounted on the dashboard under the bonnet.

Note that all correspondence concerning exported vehicles must be addressed to Nuffield Exports Limited.

Published by

THE M.G. CAR COMPANY LIMITED
Proprietors : Morris Motors Ltd.
ABINGDON-ON-THAMES
Telephone : Abingdon 251-2-3-4   Telegrams : Emgee, Abingdon

Sole Exporters:

NUFFIELD EXPORTS LIMITED
Proprietors : Morris Motors Ltd.

COWLEY   ·   OXFORD   ·   ENGLAND

| Telephone : | Telex : | Cables : |
| Oxford, England, 77733 | Morex, Oxford, England | Morex, Oxford, England |

THE M.G. MIDGET
(Series TF and TF 1500)

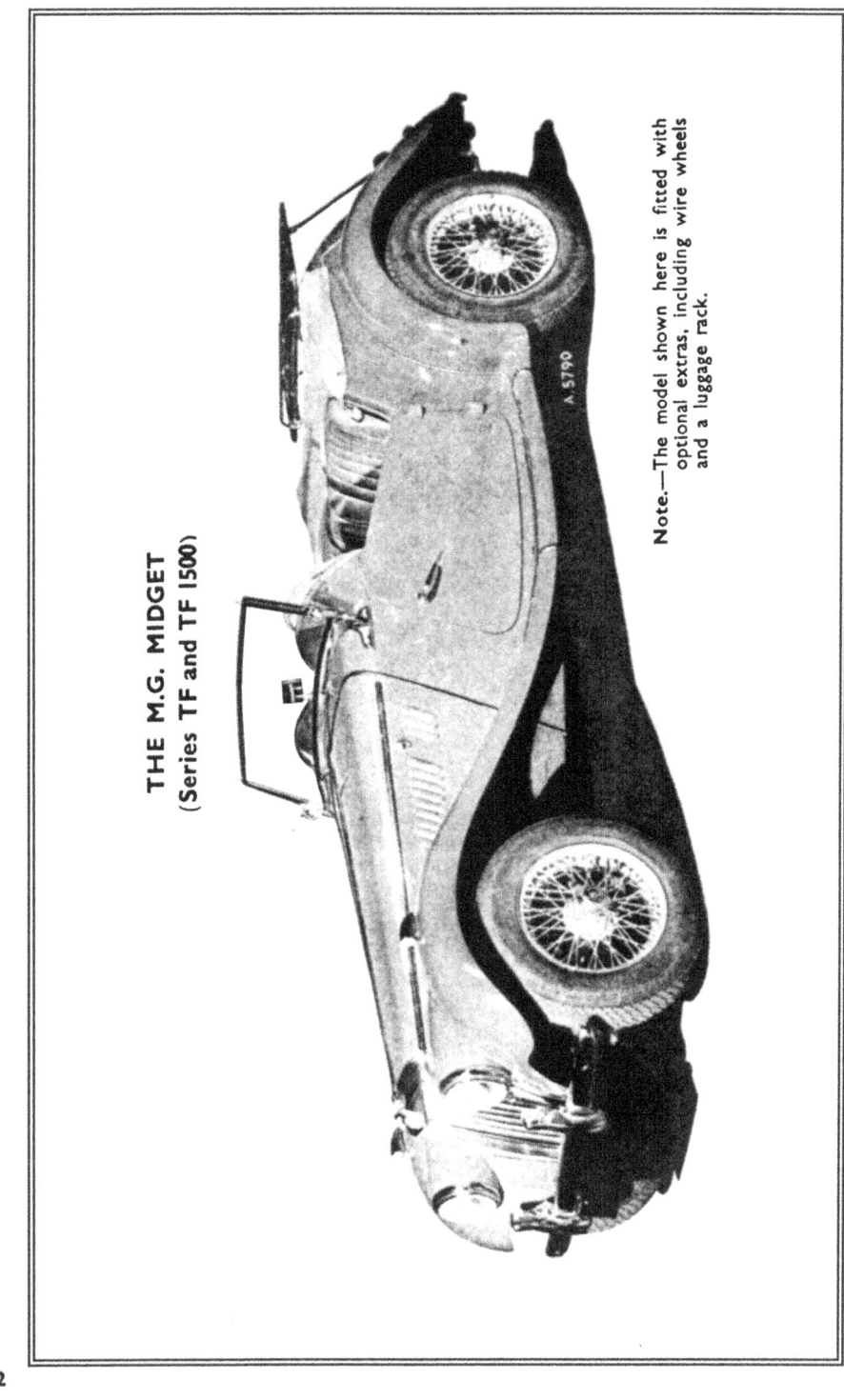

Note.—The model shown here is fitted with optional extras, including wire wheels and a luggage rack.

FOREWORD

THE information contained in this Operation Manual has been confined to the essentials necessary for the proper running and driving of the car. Nevertheless, the owner will find all the information required to maintain the car in first-class condition and to enable him to give it those all-important items of attention which go so far to ensure trouble-free and satisfactory service.

Every car leaving the Works is capable of giving absolute satisfaction if attention is given to the essential maintenance operations detailed in this book. Remember that M.G. Distributors/Dealers are better equipped to provide routine and repair service than the owner-driver; therefore, if you encounter trouble consult the Distributor or Dealer or the Service Department of The M.G. Car Company Limited—they are at your service.

An exchange scheme for many major items and assemblies is run by B.M.C. Service Limited; ask your Distributor or Dealer for details.

For those requiring information of a more detailed and technical nature than is contained in the Operation Manual a Workshop Manual is available at a reasonable price from your Distributor or Dealer.

IDENTIFICATION

When communicating with the Company or your Distributor/Dealer always quote the car and engine numbers; the registration number is of no use and is not required.

Note that all correspondence concerning exported cars must be addressed to Nuffield Exports Limited.

GENERAL DATA

	TF	TF 1500
Engine	4-cylinder overhead valve	4-cylinder overhead valve
Bore	2·618 in. (66·5 mm.)	2·835 in. (72 mm.)
Stroke	3·543 in. (90 mm.)	3·543 in. (90 mm.)
Capacity	1250 c.c. (76·28 cu. in.)	1466 c.c. (89·46 cu. in.)
R.A.C. rating ...	10·97 h.p.	12·33 h.p.
Firing order	1, 3, 4, 2	1, 3, 4, 2
Tappet clearance ...	·012 in. (hot) (·30 mm.)	·012 in. (hot) (·30 mm.
Sparking plugs ...	Champion NA8, 14 mm., ¾ in. reach	Champion NA8, 14 mm., ¾ in. reach
Sparking plug gap ...	·020 to ·022 in. (·5 to ·56 mm.)	·020 to ·022 in. (·5 to ·56 mm.)
Rear axle ratio ...	8/39	8/39
Overall gear ratios:		
First	17·06	17·06
Second	10·09	10·09
Third	6·752	6·752
Fourth	4·875	4·875
Reverse	17·06	17·06
Tyre size	5·50—15	5·50—15
Tyre pressures:		
Fully equipped, two up	Front: 18 lb./sq. in. (1·27 kg. cm.²) Rear: 18 lb./sq. in. (1·27 kg. cm.²)	Front and rear: 18 lb./sq. in. (1·27 kg. cm.²)
Competition and fast driving		24 lb./sq. in. (1·69 kg. cm.²)
Dimensions:		
Track (disc wheels)	Front: 47⅜ in. (1·20 m.) Rear: 50 in. (1·27 m.)	Front: 47⅜ in. (1·20 m.) Rear: 50 in. (1·27 m.)
Track (wire wheels)	Front: 48 3/16 in. (1·22 m.) Rear: 50 13/16 in. (1·29 m.)	Front: 48 3/16 in. (1·22 m.) Rear: 50 13/16 in. (1·29 m.)
Turning circle ...	31 ft. 3 in. (9·53 m.)	31 ft. 3 in. (9·53 m.)
Toe-in	Nil	Nil
Wheelbase ...	7 ft. 10 in. (2·39 m.)	7 ft. 10 in. (2·39 m.)
Length (overall) ...	12 ft. 3 in. (3·73 m.)	12 ft. 3 in. (3·73 m.)
Width (overall) front	4 ft. 11 in. (1·50 m.)	4 ft. 11 in. (1·50 m.)
Width (overall) rear	4 ft. 11¾ in. (1·52 m.)	4 ft. 11¾ in. (1·52 m.)
Height (overall), hood up	4 ft. 4½ in. (1·33 m.)	4 ft. 4½ in. (1·33 m.)
Ground clearance	6 in. (15 cm.)	6 in. (15 cm.)
Unladen weight (ready for road)	17¼ cwt. (876 kg.)	17¼ cwt. (876 kg.)
Capacities:		
Fuel tank	12 gallons (14·4 U.S. gallons—54 litres)	12 gallons (14·4 U.S. gallons—54 litres)
Fuel tank—reserve	2 gallons (2·4 U.S. gallons—9 litres)	2 gallons (2·4 U.S. gallons—9 litres)
Cooling system ...	10¼ pints (12·25 U.S. pints—5·7 litres)	10¼ pints (12·25 U.S. pints—5·7 litres)
Engine sump ...	10½ pints (12·6 U.S. pints—6 litres)	10½ pints (12·6 U.S. pints—6 litres)
Gearbox	1¼ pints (1·5 U.S. pints—·7 litre)	1¼ pints (1·5 U.S. pints—·7 litre)
Rear axle	2¼ pints (2·7 U.S. pints—1·28 litres)	2¼ pints (2·7 U.S. pints—1·28 litres)

Lamp bulbs—see page 56.

FILLING UP WITH FUEL

The quantity of fuel in the tank can readily be seen through the large filler which is situated on the left-hand side of the fuel tank at the rear of the car. Depress the small lever to release the cap and a downward pressure on the cap will suffice to close it. Tank capacity 12 gallons (54 litres). A warning light on the instrument panel is switched on when the supply drops to approx. 2 gallons (9 litres). (See page 14.)

FILLING THE COOLING SYSTEM

The radiator should be filled to approximately ½ in. (13 mm.) below the bottom of the filler neck. **Unscrew the filler cap slowly if it is being removed while the engine is hot.** The filler cap is retained by a bayonet catch with a graduated cam which permits release of internal pressure prior to removal. A lobe on the end of the cam guards against accidental release of the cap before the internal pressure is relieved. **Protect your hand against escaping steam.**

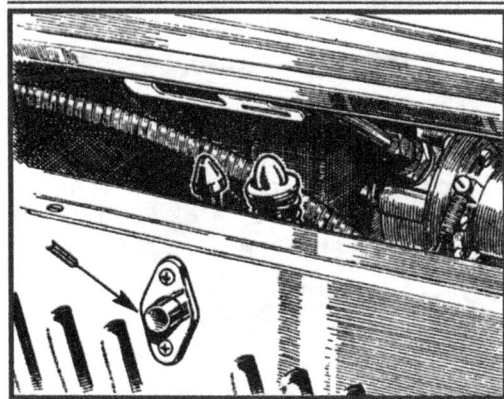

RELEASING THE BONNET

The bonnet is in two halves, opening along the centre-line of the car. Two push-buttons are provided on each side of the bonnet and these should be pressed inwards to release the bonnet catches.

PREPARING FOR THE ROAD

Checking Engine Oil Level
Filling Up with Engine Oil · Gloveboxes

CHECKING ENGINE OIL LEVEL
Check the supply of oil in the sump by withdrawing the dipstick on the left-hand side of the cylinder block. Wipe the lower portion of the rod, re-insert it and withdraw it again. Oil will cling to the rod and show the actual quantity present in the sump. The normal oil level is indicated by the 'FULL' mark on the dipstick. The engine must not be run for long periods when the oil level has dropped below the 'HALF' mark.

FILLING UP WITH ENGINE OIL
The filling orifice is on the top of the valve mechanism cover. To open pull the small knob upwards and remove the cap. To lock the cap in position press the small knob downwards. Make sure the cap is properly locked.
Clean fresh oil is essential and for a list of recommended lubricants see page 64. For sump draining instructions see page 32.

GLOVEBOXES
Two gloveboxes are provided, one on each side of the instrument panel. When a radio is fitted the set and control panel can occupy one of the gloveboxes.

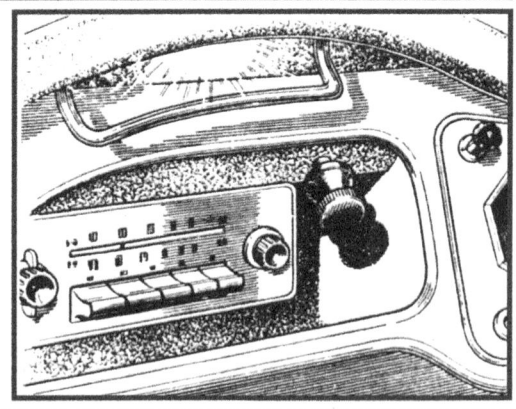

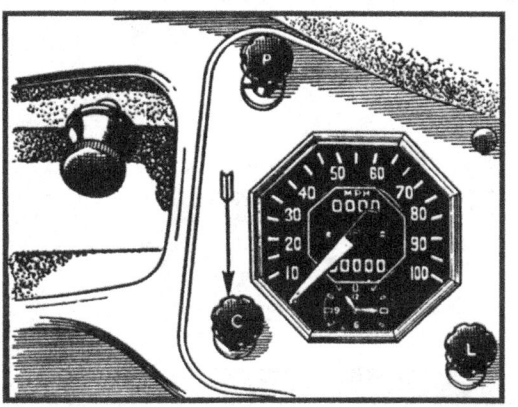

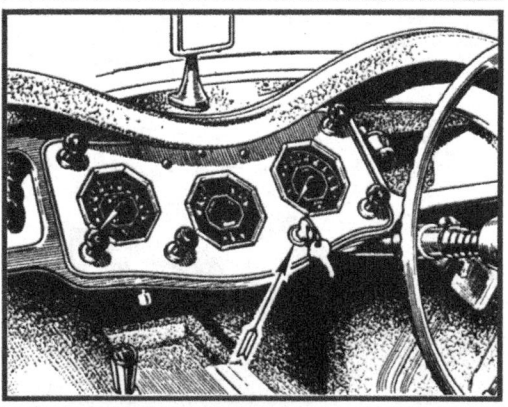

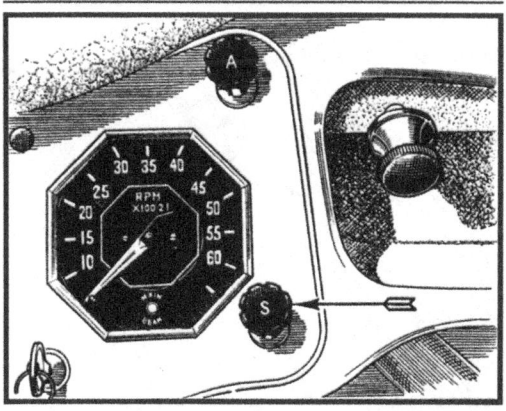

STARTING UP

Engine cold. See that the gear lever is in its neutral position. Pull out the mixture control knob marked 'C' and turn it 90° anti-clockwise to lock it in position.

Switch on the ignition by inserting the key and turning it clockwise. Pull out smartly the starter switch knob marked 'S'. The engine should revolve and start.

Release the starter switch immediately the engine fires.

Gradually return the mixture control knob to the 'off' position as soon as the warming engine will allow. (See note on starter operation on page 11.)

Engine hot. See that the gear lever is in its neutral position. Switch on the ignition by inserting the key and turning it clockwise. Pull out the starter switch knob smartly, when the engine should revolve and start. Release the starter switch immediately the engine fires.

PREPARING FOR THE ROAD
Warming Up · Running In
Hand Brake

WARMING UP
It is extremely bad practice to allow the engine to warm up from cold by letting it idle slowly. The correct procedure is to let the engine turn over fairly fast (approximately 1,000 r.p.m., corresponding to a speed of 15 m.p.h. or 24 km.p.h. in top gear), so that it attains its correct working temperature as **quickly as possible.**

RUNNING IN
It is a great mistake to drive a new car either fast or hard (such as labouring up inclines on top gear). **For the first 200 miles (320 km.) 35 m.p.h. (56 km.p.h.) must not be exceeded in top gear, 26 m.p.h. (42 km.p.h.) in third gear, 15 m.p.h. (24 km.p.h.) in second gear or 10 m.p.h. (16 km.p.h.) in bottom gear.** Engine speeds should then only be increased gradually and progressively. At least 3,000 miles (5000 km.) should be covered before running on full throttle.

HAND BRAKE
The hand brake lever is located between the two seat cushions. To operate, pull up and depress the thumb-operated knob to lock the lever in position. To release, pull upwards on the lever, when the ratchet will automatically release itself. The hand brake is automatically adjusted at the same time as the rear hydraulic brakes, and needs no separate adjustment. The nuts at the base of the lever **must not be disturbed.**

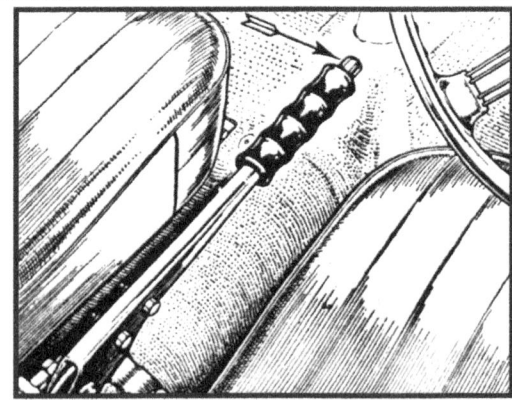

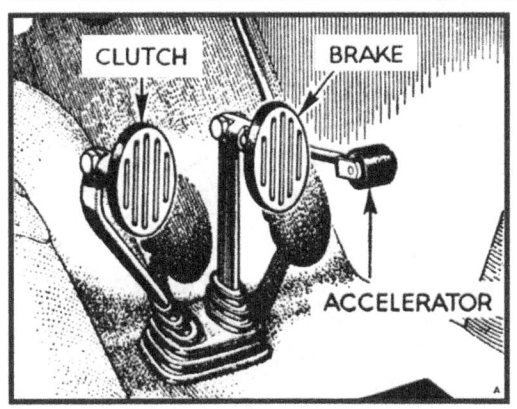

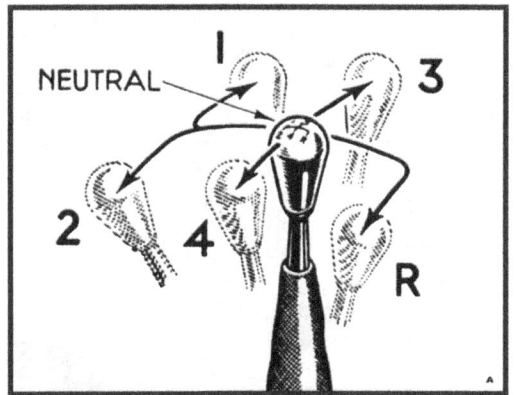

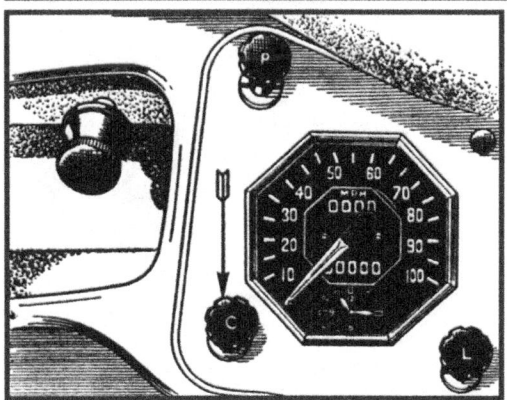

PEDAL CONTROLS

The pedal controls are arranged in the orthodox positions, namely the clutch pedal, brake pedal and accelerator, reading from left to right. Do not drive with your foot resting on the clutch pedal. It is bad practice and leads to rapid wear in the operating mechanism.

GEAR LEVER

The gear lever is centrally situated. First and second gears are selected by moving the lever to the left, and engaged by moving it forward for first gear and backwards for second gear. Third and fourth gears are selected by moving the lever to the right through the neutral position then forwards for third gear and backwards for fourth gear. To engage the reverse gear move the lever to the right of the neutral position until resistance is felt, apply side pressure to the lever to overcome the resistance and then move it backwards to engage the gear. Synchromesh engagement is provided on second, third and fourth gears.

MIXTURE CONTROL

The mixture control marked 'C' can be drawn out to give a rich mixture for starting purposes. It is locked in the open position by turning it anti-clockwise through 90°.

On no account should the engine be run for any length of time with the knob in this position. It should be returned to the 'off' position as soon as possible. A little practice will soon familiarize the driver with the correct use of this control.

DRIVING CONTROLS
Ignition Switch
Ignition Warning Light · Starter Switch

IGNITION SWITCH

The ignition switch is located on the right-hand side of the panel and is operated by a removable key. Turn the key clockwise to switch on.

Do not let the switch remain in the 'on' position when the engine is stationary, except for short periods.

IGNITION WARNING LIGHT

The ignition warning light glows red when the ignition is switched on. It will go out when the dynamo is charging adequately. It will glow red if the dynamo is not delivering sufficient current. The light may glow when the engine is idling in traffic, but no harm will be done so long as the engine is running. On no account must it be allowed to glow for more than a few moments with the car and engine stationary. Switch off the ignition immediately.

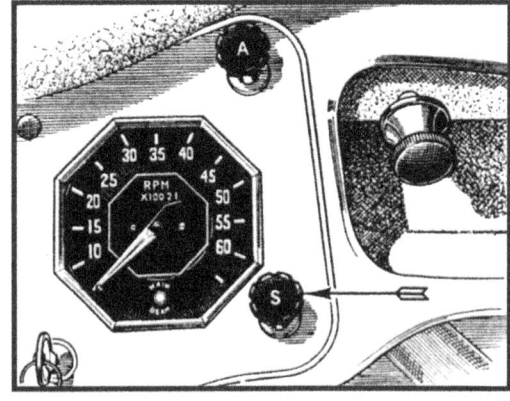

STARTER SWITCH

The starter switch is operated when the knob marked 'S' is pulled outwards. The control must be released immediately the engine fires. Operate the knob smartly in both directions. See page 11 for information on the proper use of this switch.

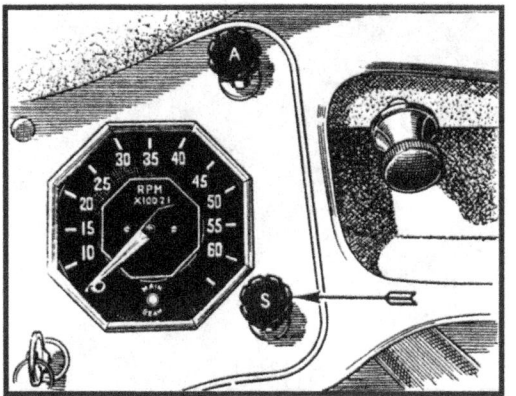

WHEN USING THE STARTER

Observe the following points :

(1) See that the controls are properly set.

(2) Operate the starter switch firmly and release it as soon as the engine fires.

(3) Do not operate the starter when the engine is running. If the engine will not fire at once, allow it to come to rest before using the switch again.

(4) Do not run the battery down by keeping the starter on when the engine will not start.

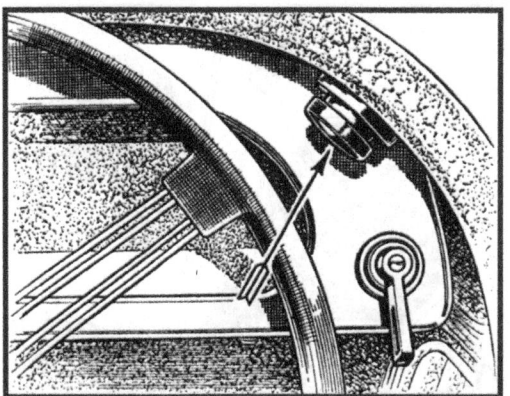

HORN BUTTON

This is the black knob located beneath the scuttle rim on the driver's side of the car.

HEADLAMP AND SIDELAMP SWITCH

The side- and headlamp switch is the control marked 'L' on the instrument panel.

Pull outwards to the first stop to operate the sidelamps, tail lamps and number-plate lamp.

Turn the knob to the right and pull out to the second position to switch on the headlamps.

SWITCHES

Dip Switch · Headlamp Beam Warning Light · Panel Light and Map Light Switch

DIP SWITCH

This is situated over the toeboard next to the clutch pedal and is foot-operated. It is of the single-acting repeating type, dipping the headlamp beams on one depression, and raising them on the next.

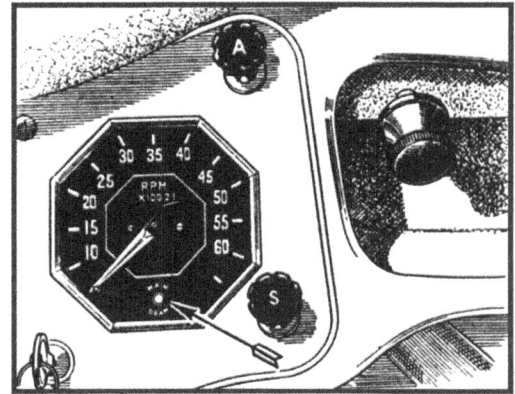

HEADLAMP BEAM WARNING LIGHT

A small bulb at the bottom of the engine revolution counter dial glows when the headlamp main beams are in the raised position. This provides visual warning to the driver to dip his headlamps for approaching traffic.

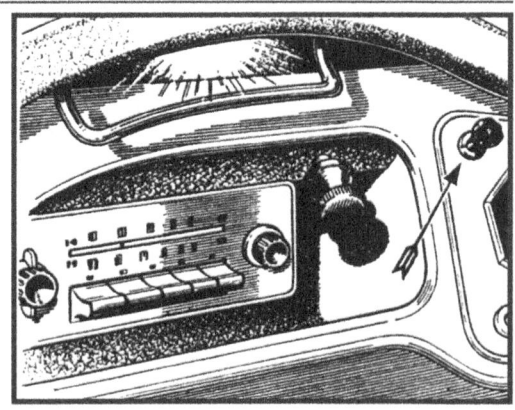

PANEL LIGHT AND MAP LIGHT SWITCH

The switch is the one marked 'P' on the instrument panel. Pull the switch knob outwards to the first stop to operate the panel lamps. Turn to the right and pull out again to operate the map lights. There is one map light over each glovebox. The lights only come on when the sidelamps also are switched on.

Auxiliary or Fog Lamp Switch · Windscreen
Wiper Switch · Direction Indicator Switch

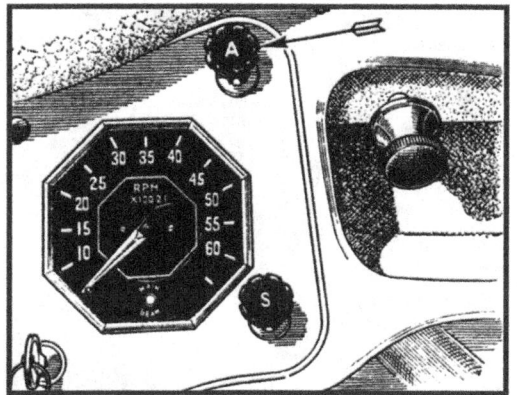

AUXILIARY OR FOG LAMP SWITCH

To enable a fog lamp to be fitted a switch is provided, which is already wired into the cable harness.

The switch is marked 'A' and is on the right of the panel. The lamp will operate only when the switch is pulled outwards while the sidelamps are on. **Remember it is illegal within the United Kingdom to use the fog lamp except in conditions of fog or falling snow.**

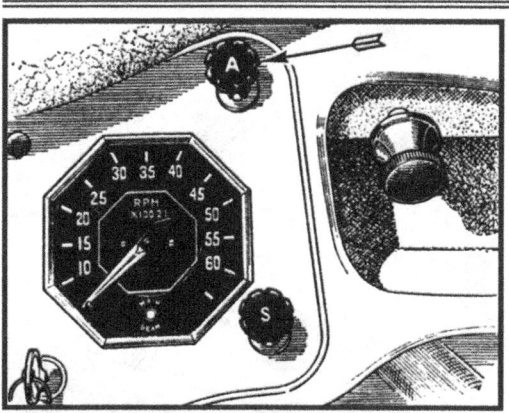

WINDSCREEN WIPER SWITCH

To operate the wipers, push forwards the control knob in front of the driver and turn towards the centre of the car. Release the knob to engage the drive. The passenger's blade is engaged in the same way but will only operate if the driver's blade is working. To switch off the motor and park the blades, push the knobs forward and turn outwards.

The windscreen wipers operate only when ignition is switched on.

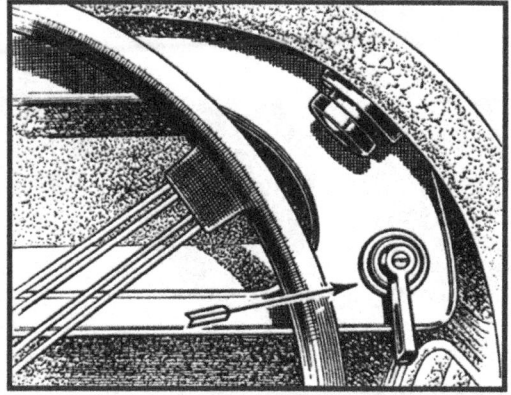

DIRECTION INDICATOR SWITCH

The lever-type time switch on the outer edge of the fascia panel controls the flashing light direction indicator unit. The unit will operate only while the ignition is switched on and flashes the sidelamp and tail lamp on the side to which the switch lever is moved until automatically switched off. While the flashing unit is switched on the right-hand warning light on the instrument panel will show green.

WARNING LIGHTS AND GAUGES
Fuel Light · Flashing Unit Warning · Water Temperature · Ammeter · Oil Pressure

FUEL WARNING LIGHT

This small light is the left-hand one at the top of the instrument panel, and glows blue when the quantity of fuel in the tank has fallen to approximately 2 gallons (9 litres), giving warning that the fuel supply is getting low.

FLASHING UNIT WARNING LIGHT

This is the right-hand one above the centre of the instrument panel. It glows green when the flashing unit is operating.

AMMETER

This instrument shows the rate at which the battery is being charged or discharged. When the dynamo is supplying more current than is required the ammeter will show the charging rate. A discharge will be shown if the demand of the equipment switched on is greater than the dynamo output. When battery is fully charged the charging rate will be low, due to the functioning of the automatic voltage control. This gives an indication of the condition of the battery.

PRESSURE AND TEMPERATURE GAUGES

The oil gauge shows the pressure of the oil which is being delivered by the oil pump and indicates that the pump is functioning correctly. A pressure between 25 and 40 lb. (1·75 and 2·8 kg./cm.²) is shown under normal running conditions. A lower figure is shown when the engine is running slowly. The temperature gauge indicates the cooling water temperature, which should be from 80 to 90° C.

Speedometer · Clock · Revolution Indicator
Starting Handle · Jack

PRESS AND TURN

SPEEDOMETER AND CLOCK

The speedometer has both trip and total mileage recorders. The trip recorder is reset to zero by a knob adjacent to the glovebox lower corner. Press the small knob and turn it until the figures read zero.

There is a small clock below the speedometer which is set by passing fingers through the hole beneath the instrument panel to reach the knob on the back-plate of the clock. Press the knob inwards and turn.

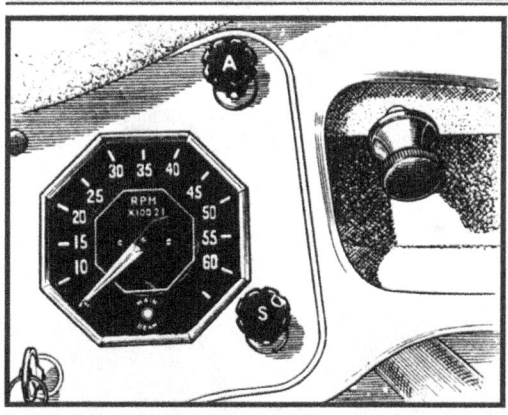

REVOLUTION INDICATOR

This indicates the engine speed. The indicator is marked in divisions of a hundred revolutions.

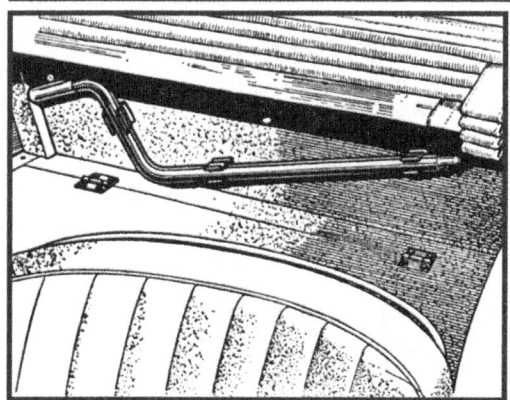

STARTING HANDLE, JACK AND TOOL KIT

The starting handle is located in spring clips on the back of the luggage compartment. The jack and tool kit are stowed in a compartment under the bonnet. The tool box may be reached from either side of the car.

A list of tools is given on p. 16.

DRIVING ADJUSTMENTS
Seat Adjustment
Steering Column Adjustment · Tool Kit

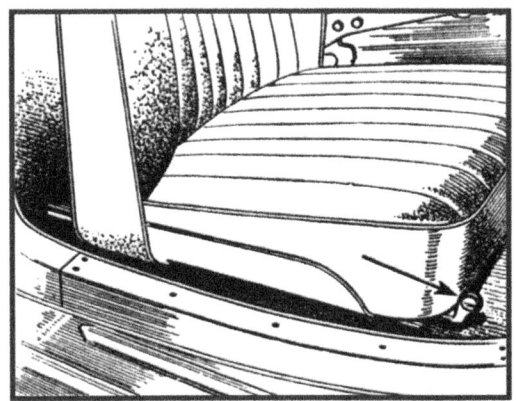

SEAT ADJUSTMENT
A lever is provided at the outside corner of each seat and must be pressed outwards to release the catches and allow the seat to slide to the required position.

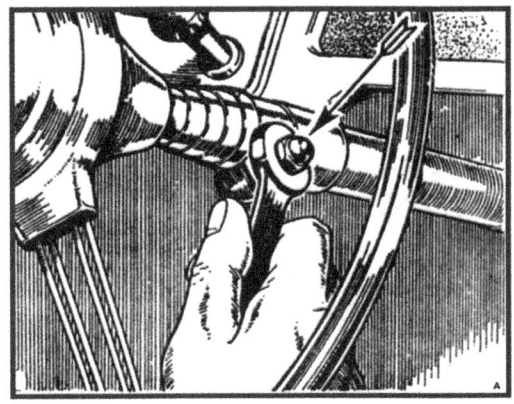

STEERING COLUMN
This is adjustable for length by slackening off the dome-headed nut and moving the wheel along the splines as required.
Do not forget to retighten the nut.

TOOL KIT
A comprehensive set of tools is provided as detailed below :

Ring-type tappet spanner.
Wheel brace (pressed wheels) or copper hammer (wire wheels).
Tappet feeler gauge—·012 in. (·30 mm.).
$\frac{3}{4}$ lb. hammer.
Pair of pliers.
Grease gun.
Tool roll.
Adjustable spanner.
Two tyre levers.

Tyre valve spanner.
Distributor feeler and screwdriver.
Tyre pump.
Set of box spanners :
$\frac{1}{4}" \times \frac{5}{16}"$, $\frac{3}{8}" \times \frac{7}{16}"$, $\frac{1}{2}" \times \frac{9}{16}"$ and tommy-bar.
Set of open spanners :
$\frac{1}{4}" \times \frac{5}{16}"$, $\frac{3}{8}" \times \frac{7}{16}"$, $\frac{1}{2}" \times \frac{9}{16}"$.
Screwdriver.
Jack and jack handle.
Lockheed bleeder drain tube.

(The tools supplied may vary or be omitted from time to time as a result of the steel supply situation or design modifications.)

MAINTENANCE ATTENTION
Valve Tappet Clearance
Clutch Pedal Clearance and Adjustment

TAPPET CLEARANCES

Both inlet and exhaust valves should have a clearance of at least ·012 in. (·30 mm.) when hot. It is of utmost importance to set No. 1 valve with No. 8 fully open

No. 3	,,	,,	No. 6	,,	,,
No. 5	,,	,,	No. 4	,,	,,
No. 2	,,	,,	No. 7	,,	,,
No. 8	,,	,,	No. 1	,,	,,
No. 6	,,	,,	No. 3	,,	,,
No. 4	,,	,,	No. 5	,,	,,
No. 7	,,	,,	No. 2	,,	,,

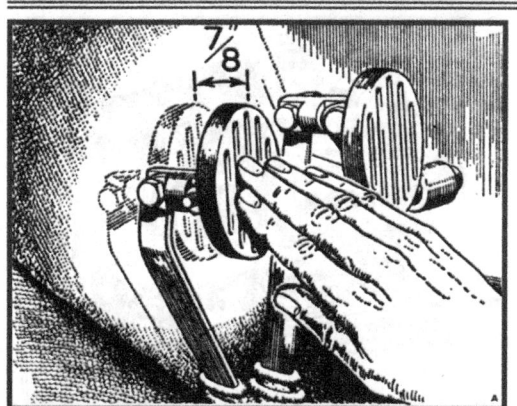

CLUTCH PEDAL CLEARANCE

It is of the utmost importance that the pedal has $\frac{7}{8}$ to 1 in. (22·2 to 25·4 mm.) minimum free travel before operating the clutch withdrawal mechanism. The free movement is easily determined by light hand pressure on the pedal.

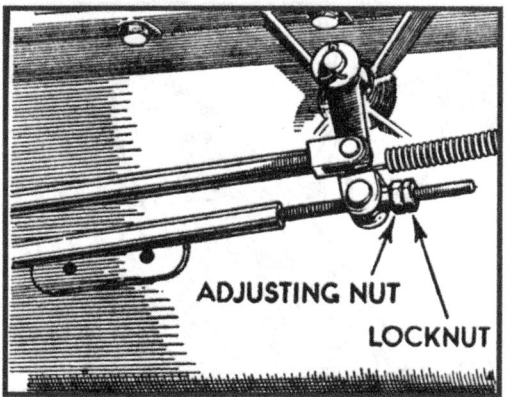

ADJUSTING NUT

LOCKNUT

CLUTCH PEDAL ADJUSTMENT

The clearance or free travel of the clutch pedal is adjusted to $\frac{7}{8}$ to 1 in. (22·2 to 25·4 mm.) by means of the nut indicated, after releasing the locknut. Check the effective travel, making sure it is not less than 3 in. (76·2 mm.).

MAINTENANCE ATTENTION

Hydraulic Dampers · Spare Wheel
Topping Up Front and Rear Dampers

HYDRAULIC DAMPERS

The hydraulic dampers fitted to the M.G. Midget are carefully set before dispatch and cannot be adjusted without special equipment.

Their design is such that they are capable of giving long service without attention beyond periodical replenishment of the fluid.

No attempt should be made to adjust or dismantle the dampers.

TOPPING UP FRONT AND REAR DAMPERS

Every 12,000 miles (20000 km.) the dampers should be removed from the car and checked for correct action. This is best entrusted to your nearest M.G. Dealer.

Only the fluid recommended and marketed by the makers of the dampers should be used. Maintain the fluid level by pouring through the filler cap indicated by the arrow.

SPARE WHEEL

This is stowed on the back of the car. The wheel disc should be removed from the pressed-type wheel to reveal the three standard wheel-fixing nuts which hold it to the carrying bracket. Remove the nuts and lift the wheel from the carrier.

To release a wire wheel, unscrew (turn anti-clockwise) the retaining wing nut by knocking the ears with the copper hammer.

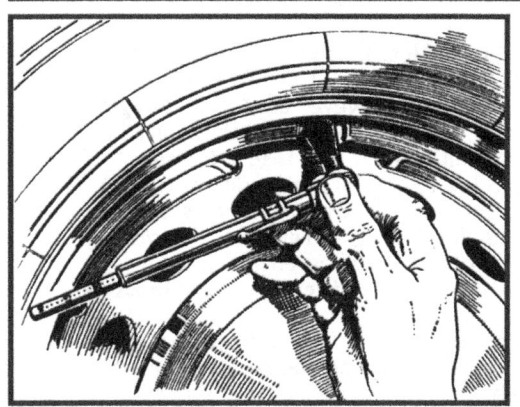

CHECKING TYRE PRESSURES

The tyre pressures should be checked and, if necessary, adjusted weekly. Gauges for testing tyre pressure can be bought from all reputable motor dealers.
The correct tyre pressures are :
Front : 18 lb./sq. in.
      (1·27 kg./cm.²).
Rear : 18 lb./sq. in.
      (1·27 kg./cm.²).

VALVE CAPS

Make sure that the valve caps are replaced and fully tightened to exclude dust and water from the valve seats. Place the caps on a clean surface while testing and inflating the tyre.
They protect the interiors and act as a secondary air seal.

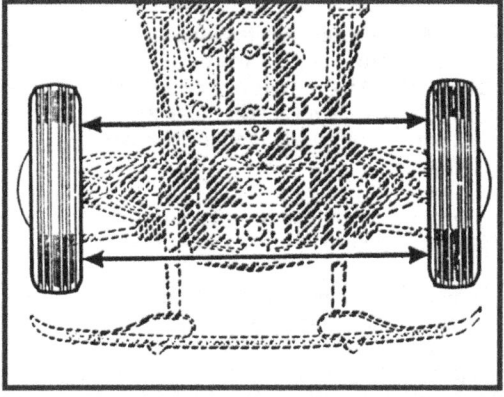

STEERING GEAR

Tracking up the wheels. Excessive and uneven tyre wear is usually caused by faulty wheel tracking. The wheels should run parallel to each other, but care must be used to ensure that the measurements are taken at axle level and that the rims run true. Correct setting of the front wheels entails the use of a wheel alignment gauge, and the owner is advised to entrust this work to an Authorized M.G. Dealer, who has the necessary equipment.

DRIVING
Gear Changing
Good Driving · Precautions

GEAR CHANGING

Start in first gear. This is engaged by declutching, moving the gear lever to the left and forward into the first gear position. Gradual release of the clutch pedal allows the car to move forward. Never use force to engage a gear. If it does not engage easily, declutch and repeat the operation. Second gear should be engaged when the car has reached a speed of approximately 6 m.p.h. (10 km.p.h.) by declutching and moving the gear lever straight back through the neutral position. The accelerator should be gently depressed as the clutch is again released, in order to take up the drive smoothly and avoid stalling the engine.

Third gear should be engaged when the car speed reaches approximately 12 m.p.h. (20 km.p.h.).

Top gear should be engaged at approximately 18 m.p.h. (30 km.p.h.). When changing up, the foot should be taken off the accelerator pedal to allow the engine to slow down.

When experience has been gained, gear changing can be carried out at considerably higher speeds with advantage, approximately 40 m.p.h. (65 km.p.h.) from third to top.

When changing down, the foot should be maintained on the accelerator pedal to allow the engine to speed up.

GOOD DRIVING

Always change down early when encountering a gradient. It is bad practice to allow an engine to labour on a hill, and the engine is unable to pick up on the lower gear if changing is left too late.

Always take your foot off the clutch pedal when you are not actually operating it. This saves clutch wear.

It is advisable to engage a lower gear when descending a steep hill, and leave the clutch engaged to obtain the advantage of the braking action of the engine. When braking, leave the clutch in engagement till a speed of approximately 6 m.p.h. (10 km.p.h.) has been reached.

Always apply the brakes gently and progressively. Violent braking throws unnecessary strain on the car and tyres, causes skidding and is dangerous. A careful driver anticipates the need for braking.

Never engage reverse gear when the car is moving forward or a forward gear when the car is moving backwards. Always bring the car to a standstill before engaging a gear which will reverse the direction of movement of the car. Do not coast with the clutch pedal depressed.

PRECAUTIONS

The hand brake is mainly a parking brake and should only be applied to keep the car stationary when parking or to hold the car while starting on a steep hill.

High-pressure washing equipment tends to cause moisture to penetrate to the brake surfaces. As a precaution, keep the hand brake fully on while washing, and dry out the brakes by applying them lightly immediately the car is driven, keeping them applied for an appreciable distance.

SIDESCREENS

The screens are stowed in a compartment below the floor of the luggage compartment. Care must be taken not to damage them while they are being withdrawn from their housing. A note of the method of packing should be made to facilitate their replacement in conjunction with instructions on pages 22 and 23.

SIDESCREENS

The screens are stowed in a compartment below the floor of the luggage compartment. Care must be taken not to damage them while they are being withdrawn from their housing. A note of the method of packing should be made to facilitate their replacement in conjunction with instructions on pages 22 and 23.

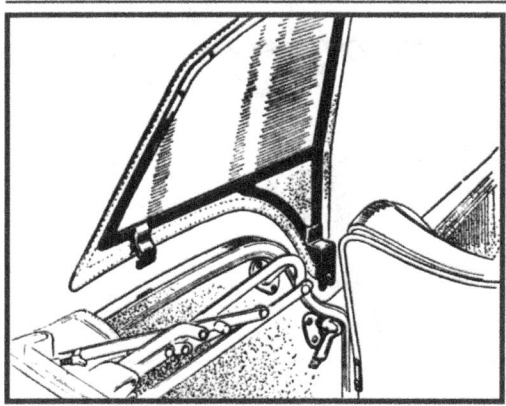

REAR SIDESCREENS

The rear sidescreens are attached to the body sides by a slotted lug engaging a socket in the upper edge of the body and by a bracket engaging a pin and wing nut at the front end.

SIDESCREEN STOWAGE
Packing Sidescreens
Step-by-step Procedure

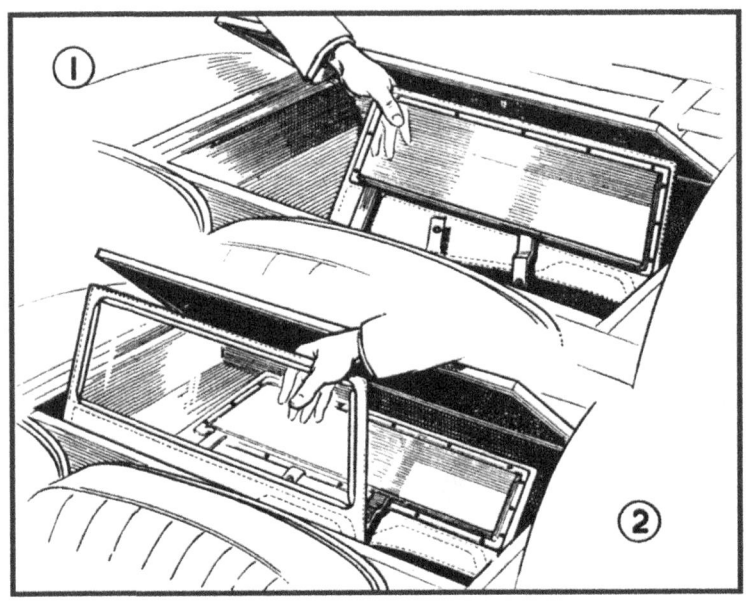

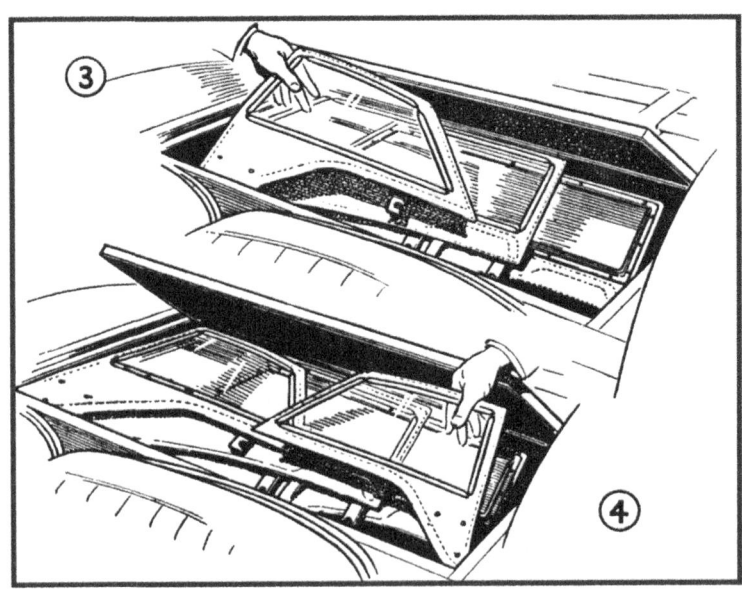

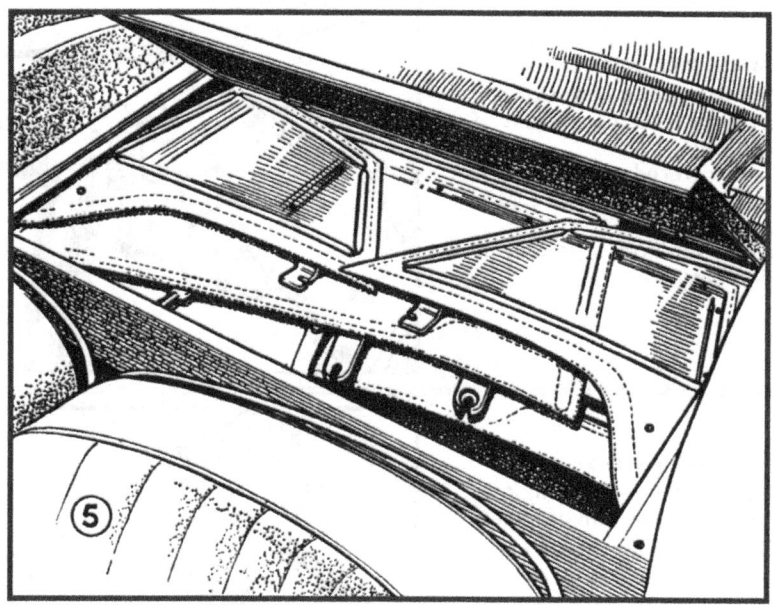

It is of the utmost importance that the sidescreens be packed together exactly as indicated, otherwise it will be found difficult to insert them into their compartment.

Start with the left-hand front sidescreen and stow it face downwards with the top edge against the rear of the stowage compartment and the front lower point against the left-hand wheel arch (1).

Place the right-hand front sidescreen on top of the left-hand one with its face side uppermost, the top edge against the rear of the stowage space and its rear edge against the right-hand wheel arch (2).

The left-hand rear sidescreen is then placed on top of the front sidescreens with its chromium-plated side uppermost and its front edge against the right-hand wheel arch (3).

Finally insert the right-hand rear sidescreen with its chromium-plated side uppermost and its front edge against the left-hand wheel arch (4).

The screens are finally stowed as shown above (5).

FOLDING THE HOOD
The Correct Method

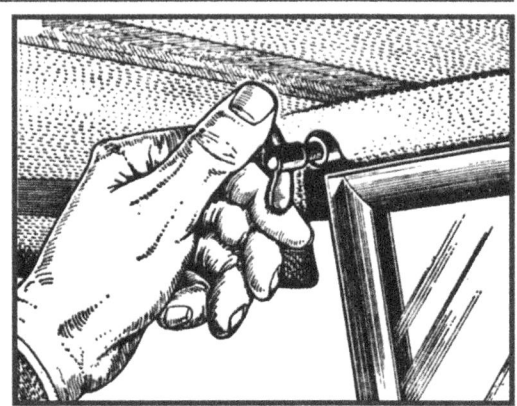

RELEASING THE HOOD

The hood is held in position on the top of the screen by means of two wing bolts.

When it is lowered it is of importance to fold it correctly to prevent damage.

The correct method of folding is detailed below.

FOLDING THE HOOD

Never fold the hood when it is wet or damp ; wait till it dries.

(1) Before folding the hood back, release the press buttons at each side. Make sure that no hood material is trapped between the hoodsticks, and that the rear panel of the hood is pulled forward.

(2) Fold the hoodsticks right down and gently pull the hood material out.

(3) Now fold the two corners in at right angles, and fold the hood as illustrated.

(4) The hood material is then folded again as shown and is ready for the tonneau cover to be fitted.

CLEANING THE HOOD

When necessary, the hood cloth may be cleaned with water applied with a brush without impairing its waterproof qualities.

Soaps must **not** be used.

UPHOLSTERY

The upholstery should be cleaned at regular intervals by wiping it with a damp cloth and polishing it with a clean soft cloth when it is dry. Do not use detergents or caustic soaps for cleaning leather upholstery.

The use of polish is quite unnecessary.

JACKING UP (REAR)

The screw-type jack should be placed under the rear spring, close to the axle, when lifting the rear of the car.

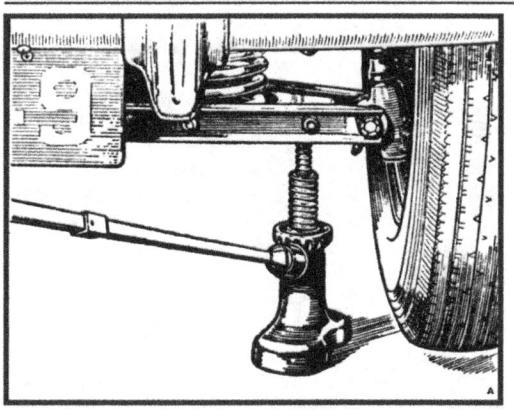

JACKING UP (FRONT)

The screw-type jack should be placed under the lower wishbones, with its pad engaging the depression between the spring seating and the lower link.

WHEELS AND TYRES
Road Wheel Disc Removal
Pressed Wheel Removal · Wire Wheels

REMOVING THE WHEEL DISCS
Remove the wheel disc by inserting the flattened end of the wheel nut spanner in the recess provided in the road wheel and levering off the hub cover, using a sideways motion of the spanner and not a radial one. A radial movement of the spanner will open out the rim of the disc.

To refit the hub disc, the rim should be placed over two of the buttons on the wheel centre and the outer face given a sharp blow with the fist over the third button.

REMOVING PRESSED WHEELS
Slacken the five nuts securing the road wheels to the hub. The wheel nuts have right-hand threads, i.e. turn clockwise to tighten and anti-clockwise to loosen. Raise the car to lift the wheel clear of the ground and remove the nuts. Withdraw the road wheel from the hub.

Reverse this procedure when replacing the road wheel and ensure that the securing nuts are tight. Every 1,000 miles check the wheel securing nuts for tightness.

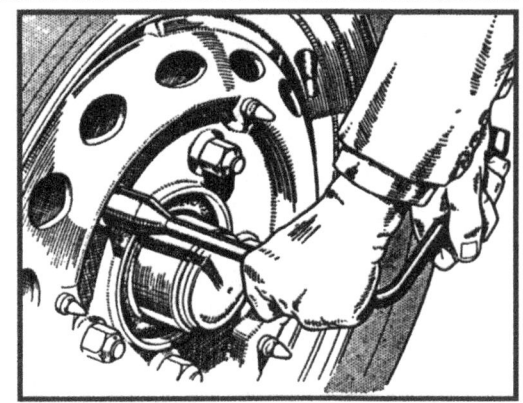

REMOVING WIRE WHEELS
Use the copper mallet provided in the tool kit to slacken the winged hub nut used to secure the wire wheel to its splined shaft. The hub nuts on the left-hand side of the car have right-hand threads (turn anti-clockwise to unscrew) and the nuts on the right-hand side of the car have left-hand threads (turn clockwise to unscrew).

A right-hand wheel is shown in the illustration.

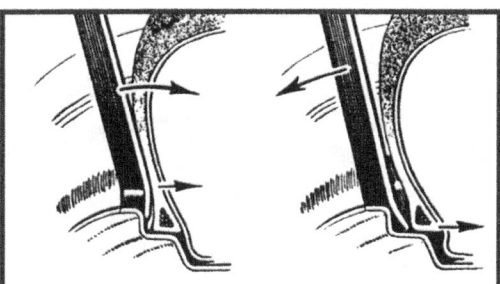

1. Insert lever between bead and rim with curved end against tyre. Press lever towards tyre.
2. Insert second lever in space between bead and rim, with curved end outwards, and pull lever away from tyre. Repeat at intervals round tyre until bead is free. Several circuits of tyre may be necessary.

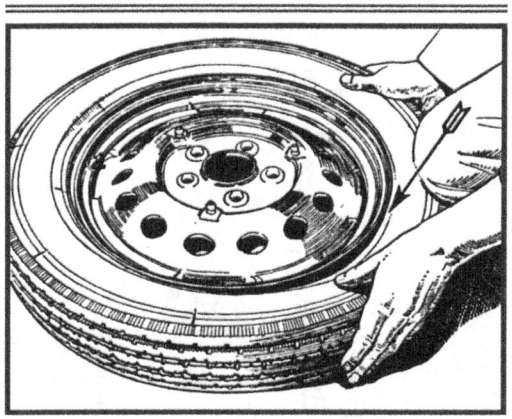

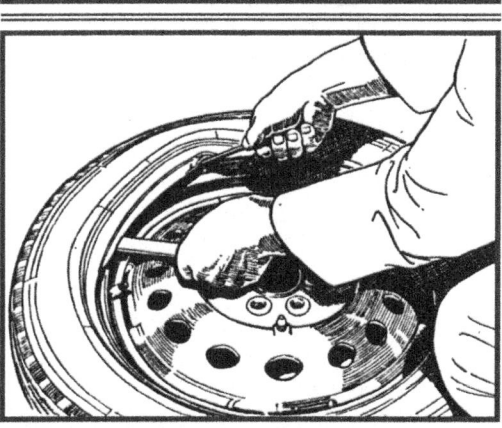

TYRE REMOVAL

Inextensible wires are incorporated in the edges of tyres. Do not attempt to stretch the edges of the tyre cover over the rim. Force is entirely unnecessary and dangerous, as it merely tends to damage the cover edges. Fitting or removing will be quite easy if the wire edges are carefully adjusted into the rim base. If the cover edge fits tightly on the rim seating it should be freed by using the tyre levers as indicated.

Remove all valve parts to completely deflate the tyre and push both cover edges into the base of the rim at the point diametrically opposite to the valve, then lever the cover edge near the valve over the rim edge (see illustration below).

This permits the tyre valve to be pushed through the hole in the rim and the inner tube to be withdrawn for attention when required.

TYRE REPLACEMENT

A similar technique has to be employed when replacing the tyre, first fitting the tyre into the rim at a point opposite to the valve, and finishing the fitting in the region of the valve, keeping the beaded edge in the well-base of the rim.

REPAIRING TUBES

Have punctures or injuries vulcanized. Ordinary patches should only be used for emergencies. Vulcanizing is absolutely essential in the case of tubes manufactured from synthetic rubber.

WHEELS AND TYRES

Tyre Valves · Valve Caps

TYRE VALVES
The airtightness of the valve depends upon the proper functioning of its interior. It may be tested for airtightness by rotating the wheel until the valve is at the top and inserting its end in an eggcup full of water. If bubbles appear the interior is faulty and should be replaced by a new one.

VALVE INTERIORS
It is advisable always to have spare interiors handy, and these are procurable suitably packed in small metal containers. A small extracting and fitting tool is supplied in the tool kit.
Always make sure that valve interiors are screwed well home on replacement.

VALVE CAPS
The valve caps should be kept firmly tightened to prevent dust and water entering and damaging the valve seats. The caps also act as an additional air seal.
When they are removed for tyre inflation or removal they should always be placed in a clean place.

Wire wheels will require periodic checking to see that no spokes have worked loose or are losing their tension.

This can be done by drawing a light spanner or similar metal object across the spokes, which should emit a clear ringing note. If any spokes are slack the note will be dull or flat by comparison.

Any small amount of individual slackness may be taken up by adjusting the spoke nipple with a spanner, but great care must be taken to ensure the general tension of the wheel is not upset by overtightening any of the spokes, as this will cause other spokes to break and the wheel to run out of truth.

If a spoke is replaced and it is found that the spoke end protrudes through the nipple body it must be filed off carefully to prevent any damage to the tyre.

Tyres should be removed periodically so that the wheel rim can be examined for corrosion.

Any signs of rust must be removed by polishing with emery-paper and the area afterwards protected with paint.

When a general overhaul of wheels becomes necessary, they should be sent to a wheel specialist for repair.

HYDRAULIC BRAKES
Brake Adjustments
Front Shoe · Rear Shoe

BRAKE ADJUSTMENTS

These are required when excessive travel of the brake pedal takes place on application.

Placing suitable blocks beneath the wheels remaining in contact with the ground, use the jack provided in the tool kit to raise each wheel of the car in turn.

The front brakes. Remove the front hub cap and road wheel and rotate the brake-drum until one of the adjustment screws is visible through one of the holes provided in the side of the brake-drum. With a screwdriver turn the screw as far as it will go in a clockwise direction until the drum is locked solid, then turn the screw anti-clockwise **one** notch only. The brake-drum should then be free to rotate without the shoes rubbing. Turn the drum until the adjustment screw diametrically opposite is visible and carry out the same procedure on this. The brake-shoes on this wheel are now fully adjusted. The brake-shoes on the other front wheel must be adjusted by the same method.

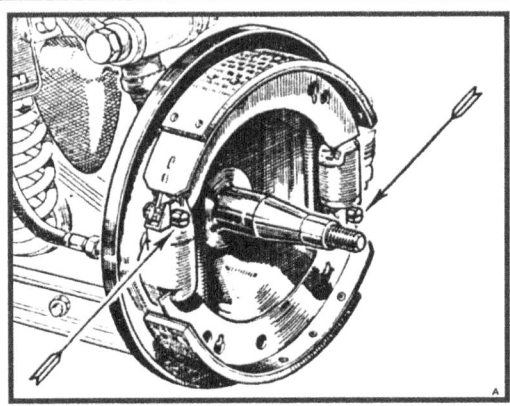

The rear brakes. The procedure is simiiar to that detailed for the front brakes, except that there is only one adjuster, which controls both brake-shoes.

It is essential that the hand brake should be fully released while the rear brake-shoes are being adjusted. Adjustment of the rear brake-shoes automatically adjusts the hand brake mechanism and no separate adjustment is required.

(See note on page 31 re hand brake adjustment.)

HAND BRAKE AND SUSPENSION
Replenishing Brake Fluid · Hand Brake
Adjustment · Rear Suspension

TOPPING UP WITH FLUID
Every 1,000 miles (1600 km.) the fluid level must be checked by turning back the front floor carpet on the driver's side and removing the rubber plug from the foot well. Undo the filler plug. The fluid level should be $\frac{1}{2}$ in. (12·70 mm.) below the bottom of the filler neck, and must never be above this. Use only Lockheed Genuine Brake Fluid. This is important. In conditions of extreme cold Wagner 21 Fluid should be used overseas.

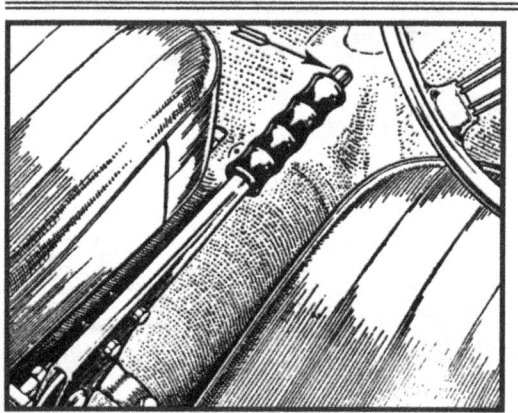

HAND BRAKE ADJUSTMENT
The hand brake operates on the rear brake-shoes and is automatically adjusted when hydraulic brake adjustment is made.
On no account must any attempt be made to adjust the hand brake cables themselves, as this will interfere with the hydraulic brakes.
The ratchet only comes into operation when the press button on the end of the lever is depressed and is automatically released when the brake lever is pulled upwards.

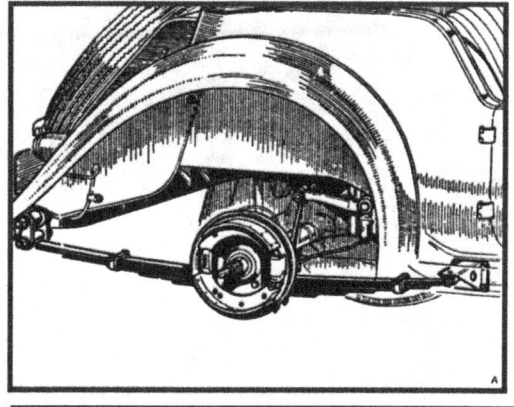

REAR SUSPENSION
The flexible laminated rear springs are mounted on rubber bushes, obviating the need for lubrication. To ensure maximum stability the axle movement is controlled by hydraulic dampers.
The rear spring 'U' bolts should be examined every 6,000 miles (10000 km.) and tightened if necessary.

LUBRICATION (Engine)
Oil Pressures • Engine Drain Plug
Replenishing Engine Sump

ENGINE LUBRICATION

The oil supply is carried in the sump below the cylinder block and is drawn through a gauze internal filter and renewable external filter before circulation through the engine. It will be found on first starting the engine from cold that a high-pressure reading will be obtained on the oil gauge. This will gradually drop as the engine warms up and the oil becomes more fluid, until a normal pressure of approximately 25 to 40 lb./sq. in. (1·75 to 2·8 kg./cm.²) is indicated. Avoid racing the engine when first starting up while the oil is cold. On the other hand, do not let it idle too slowly. It should be allowed to rotate at approximately 1,000 r.p.m., an engine speed equivalent to 15 m.p.h. (24 km.p.h.) in top gear.

Instructions for checking the quantity of oil in the sump and replenishment are given on page 6.

Only oils of the recommended makes and grades should be used.

DRAINING THE SUMP (A)

We recommend that when the car has completed the first 500 miles (800 km.) the oil in the sump should be drained to clear the sump from any impurities that may have accumulated during the initial running-in period. After the first 500 miles (800 km.) we recommend that the sump should be drained every 3,000 miles (5000 km.) and refilled with the recommended lubricant. This operation is best carried out immediately the car returns from a journey, while the oil is still warm and fluid.

On the left side of the engine will be found a brass drain plug. Removal of this plug will release the contents of the sump. After carefully cleaning the drain plug, which will probably have an accumulation of dirt in its hollow centre, it should be replaced and screwed up tightly. When the sump has been drained completely, approximately 10½ pints (6 litres) are required to fill it.

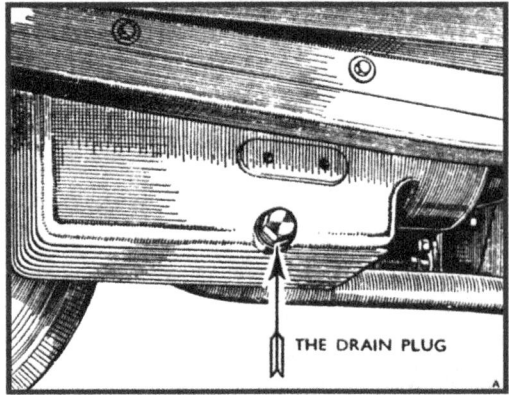

THE DRAIN PLUG

THE FILLER

GEARBOX (B)

The filler cap is located on the top of the gearbox ; a dipstick is provided on the right-hand side of the box ; they are accessible when the inspection cover has been removed.

Replenishments should take place at intervals of 1,000 miles (1600 km.), care being taken to ensure that the gearbox is not filled above the 'HIGH' mark on the dipper rod. If the level is too high, oil may get into the clutch case and cause clutch slip.

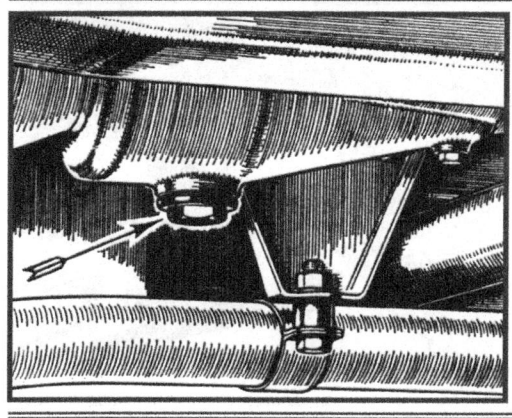

DRAINING THE GEARBOX

The gearbox should be drained after the first 500 miles (800 km.) and filled with the correct amount of the recommended lubricant. Ensure that the hollow centre of the drain plug has been cleaned thoroughly before it is replaced and tightened.

REFILLING THE GEARBOX (B)

When the gearbox has been drained completely through the plug indicated, 1¼ pints (·7 litre) of oil are required to fill it. The oil should be poured in through the filler plug shown above until it reaches the 'HIGH' mark on the dipstick. After the first 500 miles (800 km.) the gearbox should be drained and then filled with fresh oil and subsequently every 6,000 miles (10000 km.).

Use one of the oils recommended on page 64.

LUBRICATION (Rear Axle)
Rear Axle Filler and Level Plug · Rear Axle Drain Plug · Propeller Shaft Lubrication

REAR AXLE (B)

Access to the square-headed filler plug is gained when the centre section of the sidescreen stowage compartment floor has been removed. Undo the screws to lift the floor. A square-headed drain plug is fitted in the base of the differential housing and its hollow centre must be cleaned before it is replaced and tightened. The oil should be drained from the rear axle after the first 500 miles (800 km.). The axle must then be filled with one of the oils to Ref. B, page 64, to the level of the filler plug. Approximately 2¼ pints (1·3 litres) of oil are required to refill the axle.

Topping up should take place at intervals of 1,000 miles (1600 km.). The axle should be completely drained and then refilled with fresh lubricant of the correct grade every 6,000 miles (10000 km.).

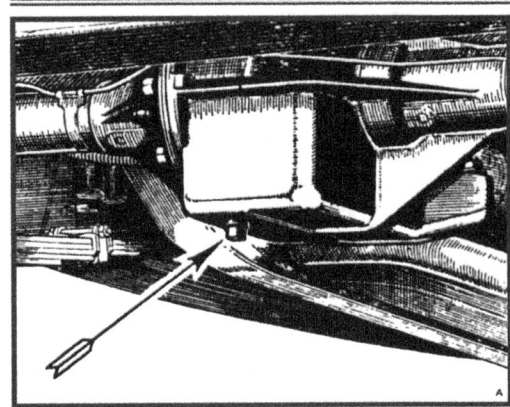

PROPELLER SHAFT (D)

The sliding joint and the two needle-type universal joints should receive grease gun attention every 1,000 miles (1600 km.). The recommended lubricants are indicated under Ref. D on page 64.

Access to the rear universal joint nipple may be gained by lifting the centre section of the sidescreen stowage compartment floor. The front universal joint must be lubricated from the under side of the car. (See page 35.)

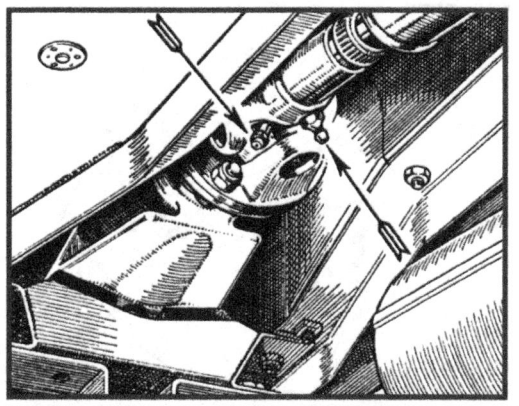

FRONT UNIVERSAL JOINT AND PROPELLER SHAFT SLIDING JOINT (D)

The lubricator for the sliding joint is indicated by the right-hand arrow. The grease gun, filled with grease to Ref. D (page 64), should be applied every 1,000 miles (1600 km.) and given three or four strokes. The grease gun should also be applied to the universal joint greaser, shown by the left-hand arrow, at the same time and given three or four strokes.

STEERING GEAR (D)

Grease nipples are provided at the top and bottom of each swivel pin. The grease gun should be filled with grease to Ref. D (page 64) and applied to the nipples every 500 miles (800 km.). Three or four strokes of the gun should be given.

STEERING GEARBOX (B)

A greaser is provided on the rack housing, and this is accessible underneath the front of the car. The nipple should be used to replenish the rack assembly with oil to Ref. B (page 64) every 3,000 miles (5000 km.). Avoid overfilling the steering gearbox. Give no more than 10 strokes of the hand gun.

LUBRICATION
Tie-rods · Front Hubs · Rear Hubs

TIE-ROD LUBRICATION (D)
Every 500 miles (800 km.) the grease gun should be applied to the nipple on the outer ends of the steering tie-rods and given three or four strokes.

The inner ball joints of the tie-rod (those within the rubber bellows) are automatically lubricated from the steering gearbox housing.

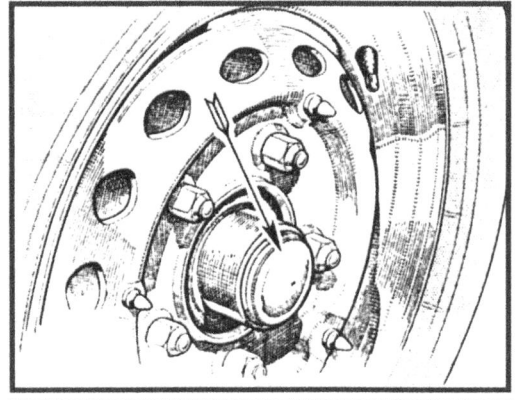

WHEEL HUBS

Front hubs (C). Every 6,000 miles (10000 km.) the front wheel hub covers should be removed and the grease-retaining cap carefully prised off the end of the hub, re-filled with grease to Ref. C (page 64), and replaced.

To lubricate the front hubs on cars fitted with wire wheels, the wheel retaining nuts must be unscrewed with the copper hammer in the tool kit and the hubs packed with grease to Ref. C every 6,000 miles (10000 km.).

Rear hubs. The rear hubs are automatically lubricated from the rear axle lubrication system and need no separate lubrication attention.

UNDO

A right-hand wheel is illustrated. The nuts undo in the opposite direction on the left-hand side.

FAN AND WATER PUMP

Every 1,000 miles (1600 km.) apply grease gun, filled with grease to Ref. C, to lubricating nipple for fan and water pump spindle and give two strokes.

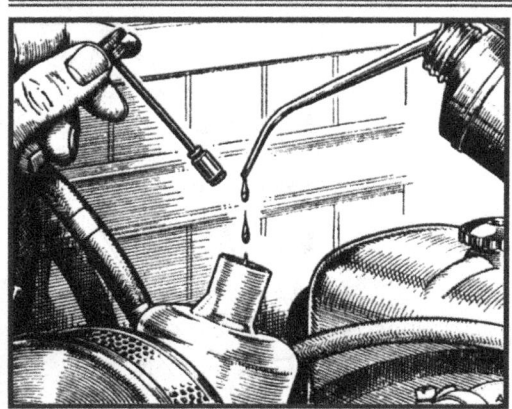

CARBURETTER DAMPERS

Every 1,000 miles (1600 km.) unscrew the oil cap at the top of each carburetter suction chamber, pour in a small quantity of engine oil to Ref. F (page 64) and replace the cap. **Under no circumstance should a heavy-bodied oil be used.** Failure to lubricate the dampers will impair the performance and reduce acceleration.

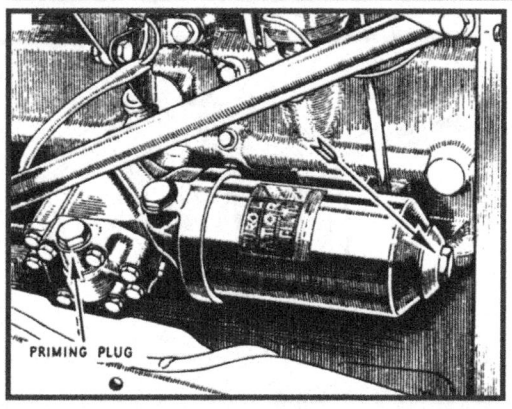

PRIMING PLUG

OIL FILTER

The main oil filter renewable element must be renewed every 6,000 miles (10000 km.). The filter is released by undoing the central bolt connecting the filter body to the filter head on the oil pump. When fitting the new element, make sure that the seating washer for the filter body is in good condition and that the body is correctly fitted.

The element is either a Purolator M.F.21 or a Tecalemit F.P.3301.

LUBRICATION
Distributor Cam · Distributor Cam Bearing
Distributor Automatic Timing Control

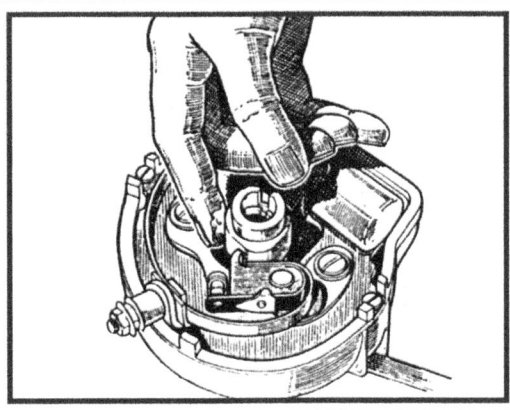

EVERY 3,000 MILES (5000 Km.) (D)
Distributor cam. Lightly smear the cam with a very small amount of grease to Ref. D (page 64), or if this is not available, clean engine oil can be used.

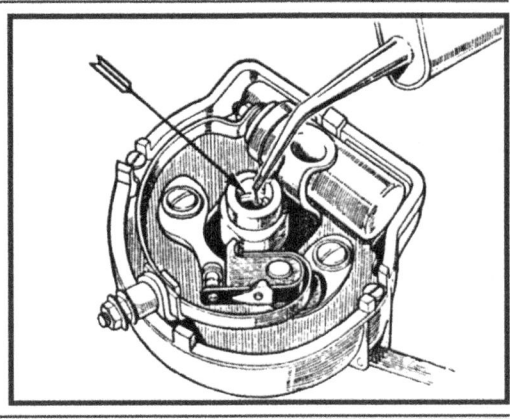

EVERY 3,000 MILES (5000 Km.) (F)
Distributor cam bearing. Lift the rotor off the top of the spindle by pulling it off squarely and add a few drops of thin engine oil (Ref. F, page 64) to the central opening. Do not remove the screw which is exposed.
There is a clearance between the screw and the inner face of the spindle for the oil to pass.
Replace the rotor with its drive lug correctly engaging the spindle slot and push it onto the shaft as far as it will go.

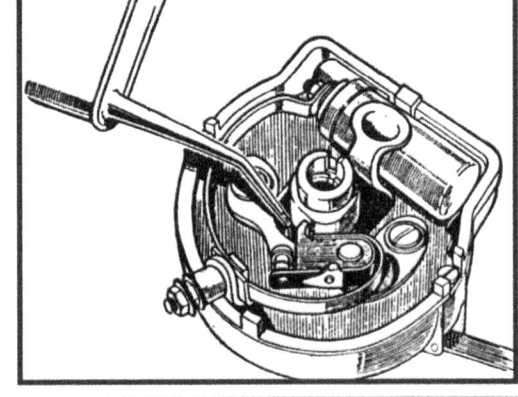

EVERY 3,000 MILES (5000 Km.) (F)
Automatic timing control. Carefully add a few drops of thin engine oil to Ref. F, page 64, through the hole in the contact breaker base through which the cam passes. Do not allow any oil to get on or near the contacts.

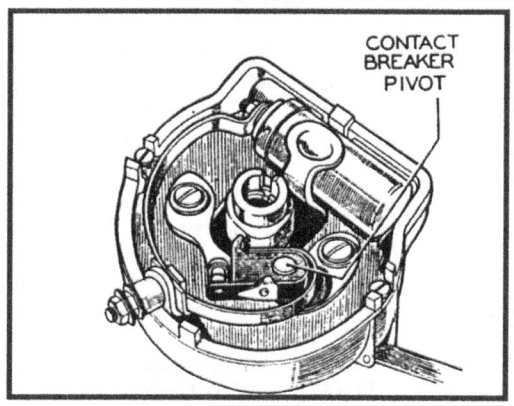

CONTACT BREAKER PIVOT

EVERY 3,000 MILES (5000 Km.) (F)
Contact breaker pivot. Place a small amount of clean engine oil to Ref. F (page 64) on the pivot on which the contact breaker lever works. Do not allow oil or grease to get on the contacts.

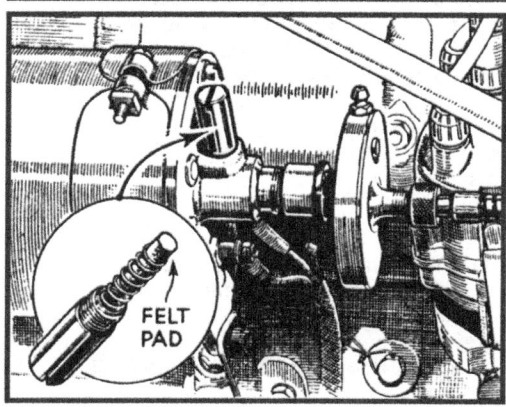

FELT PAD

EVERY 3,000 MILES (5000 Km.) (C)
Dynamo lubrication. Unscrew the lubricator fitted at the commutator end, lift out the felt pad and spring and half-fill the lubricator with high-melting-point grease to Ref. C (page 64).
Replace the spring and felt pad and screw the lubricator into position.

EVERY 6,000 MILES (10000 Km.) (B)
Apply a grease gun filled with oil to Ref. B (page 64) to revolution indicator gearbox on dynamo.

GREASE GUN
The grease gun is filled by unscrewing the large cap on the end of the container and removing the automatic feed plunger; when the gun is sufficiently full of grease replace the plunger end cap. The gun is, in effect, a high-pressure pump and it has a recessed end. By applying the recess to the grease nipples and pushing on the gun, grease is forced into the bearings.
Use the correct grease for each purpose.

PERIODICAL ATTENTION

After first 500 miles (800 km.). Drain old oil from engine ; **do not wash with paraffin** but merely fill with fresh oil. Examine valve rocker clearance and adjust if inadequate. Tighten cylinder head stud nuts. Drain old oil from gearbox and rear axle and replenish with fresh oil.

NOTE.—This service is free under the M.G. 500 Miles Free Service Scheme (see page 43).

Every 250 miles (500 km.). Inspect oil level in crankcase. Refill if necessary. (See page 6.)

Every 500 miles (800 km.). Attach grease gun to the following grease nipples and give pump three or four strokes. These nipples are situated as under :

> 2 on steering tie-rods, 4 on steering knuckles. (On L.H.D. models there is one on the clutch and brake pedal shaft in addition.)

Every 1,000 miles (1600 km.). Oil door lock bolts. Oil door hinges. Examine oil level in gearbox and rear axle ; replenish if necessary. Apply grease gun filled with grease to Ref. D (page 64) to the three grease nipples on the propeller shaft and give three or four strokes. Examine fluid level in hydraulic brake gear supply tank and replenish if necessary. The tank should never be allowed to be less than half-full of fluid or more than three-quarters full. **Use only Lockheed Genuine Fluid.**

Top up battery with distilled water. (See page 49.)

Apply grease gun filled with grease to Ref. C (page 64) to grease nipple on water pump spindle, giving two strokes.

Check tightness of wheel securing nuts.

Replenish oil in carburetter piston dashpots. (See page 37.)

Every 3,000 miles (5000 km.). Drain engine. Refill with fresh oil. (See page 32.) Give distributor rotating cam a slight smear of grease to Ref. D (page 64).

Clean and re-oil air filters (see page 44).

Remove distributor rotor and add a few drops of thin machine oil in opening. (See page 38.)

Add two drops of thin machine oil to opening round distributor rotating arm. (See page 38.)

Smear contact breaker rocker arm pivot with engine oil to Ref. F (page 64). Check contact breaker gap (page 48).

Check and clean sparking plugs (page 44).

Remove dynamo lubricator cap and refill with grease to Ref. C (page 64). Check tension of dynamo driving belt and adjust if necessary. (See page 50.) Clean fuel pump points. Clean and re-oil air cleaner.

Apply oil gun filled with oil to Ref. B (page 64) to steering gearbox grease nipple and give 10 strokes.

Every 6,000 miles (10000 km.). Drain gearbox and rear axle, refill with fresh oil. Fit new filter element to external oil filter. (See page 37.) Tighten door hinge fixing screws. Tighten rear road spring seat bolts. Clean fuel filters at carburetter and fuel pump.

Remove grease-retaining cap from front wheels, or wheel-retaining nut on models fitted with wire wheels, and replenish with grease to Ref. C.

Examine the gaps of the sparking plugs and make sure that they are not too wide ; they should be ·020 to ·022 in. (·5 to ·56 mm.). Apply grease gun filled with oil to Ref. B (page 64) to nipple on revolution indicator gearbox on dynamo. Check valve tappet clearance.

Every 12,000 miles (20000 km.). Remove sump and clean oil filter. Check fluid level in shock absorbers, refill if necessary with recommended fluid (see page 18). Replace sparking plugs with new ones. Adjust clutch pedal clearance. Check dynamo and starter brushes.

USE OF OILCAN

The owner is advised to keep an oilcan filled with a light oil to Ref. F (page 64) to apply to the bonnet lock and prop mechanism and the door locks and hinges, etc., at frequent intervals. Attention to such details ensures trouble-free action and prevents undue wear. Make sure that all points receive attention.

Regular servicing, as proved by presentation of completed voucher counterfoils, could well enhance the value of your vehicle in the eyes of a prospective purchaser.

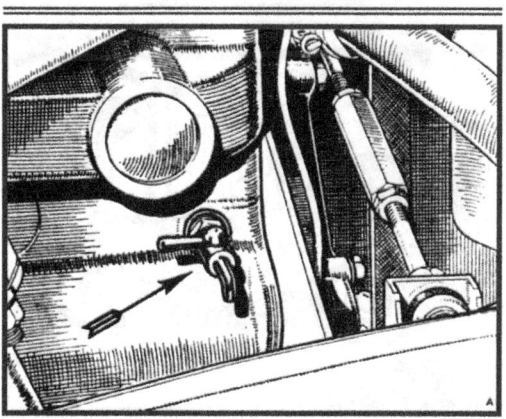

DRAINING THE COOLING SYSTEM

The radiator drain tap is fitted on the left-hand side of the radiator bottom tank, as indicated by the arrow in the top illustration.

Owing to the location of the water pump a certain amount of water is trapped in the cylinder block and cannot be drained from the radiator.

A second drain tap is therefore fitted on the right-hand side of the engine at the lowest point of the cooling passages, as indicated by the arrow in the bottom illustration.

It is essential to open this tap to drain the system completely.

COLD WEATHER PRECAUTIONS
Draining the Cooling System
Attention to Bodywork

COLD WEATHER PRECAUTIONS

If the car is not stored in a warmed building, steps must be taken to prevent the cooling water from freezing during frosty weather. Water upon freezing expands, with the result that there is a very considerable risk of bursting either the radiator or the cylinder block by the pressure generated. As a precautionary measure when frost is anticipated, the water should be drawn from the radiator and engine (see page 41) before the car is stored for the night, or, better still, an anti-freezing solution may be used in the radiator.

We recommend owners to use Bluecol, Filtrate Nevafreze, Shell Snowflake, or Esso Anti-freeze in order to protect the cooling system during frosty weather and reduce corrosion to a minimum.

The correct quantities of anti-freeze for different degrees of frost resistance in the M.G. Midget (Series TF and TF 1500) are :

7° F. (−14° C.)	0° F. (−18° C.)
15 per cent. solution	20 per cent. solution
Quantity : 1½ pints (·85 litre)	Quantity : 2 pints (1·14 litres)

If temperatures below 0° F. or −18° C. are likely to be encountered a solution of at least 25 per cent. anti-freeze must be used.

First decide what degree of frost protection is required before adding the anti-freeze to the radiator.

Before introducing anti-freeze mixture to the radiator it is advisable to clean out the cooling system thoroughly by swilling out the passages with a hose inserted in the filler cap, keeping the two drain taps open. Only top up when the cooling system is at its normal running temperature, in order to avoid losing anti-freeze due to expansion.

Make sure that the cooling system is watertight and examine all joints, replacing any defective rubber hose with new.

BODYWORK ATTENTION

The car should be washed and dried thoroughly before applying polish. The use of a good-quality non-abrasive polish is essential. Grease and tar spots must be carefully removed with a wadding pad dipped in petrol (gasoline). Chromium plating should be washed with soap and warm water only. Metal polishes or abrasives of any sort must on no account be used.

500 MILES FREE SERVICE
Early Attention Important
Items Included in Free Service

500 MILES (800 Km.) FREE SERVICE

During the early life of the car, soon after it has completed 500 miles (800 km.), you are entitled to have it inspected free of charge by the M.G. Dealer from whom you purchased it, or, if this should not be convenient, by any other M.G. Dealer by arrangement. This attention given during the critical period in the life of the car makes all the difference to its subsequent life and performance.

This service includes :

    Drain oil from engine, gearbox and rear axle, and refill.

    Oil and grease all points of the car.

    Tighten cylinder head and manifold nuts to recommended pressures.

    Check tightness of valve rocker shaft brackets to recommended pressures.

    Check tappet clearances, and reset if necessary.

    Tighten fan belt if necessary.

    Check all water connections, and tighten clips if necessary.

    Examine and clean carburetters, and reset slow-running adjustment if necessary.

    Examine, and adjust if necessary, sparking plug and distributor points.

    Check working of automatic ignition controls, and if necessary reset ignition timing.

    Check front wheel alignment and steering connections. Adjust if necessary.

    Check tightness of universal joint nuts, wheel nuts, spring clips and wing (fender) bolts.

    Check clutch pedal for free movement, and adjust if necessary.

    Check fluid level in master cylinder, and top up if necessary.

    Check braking system functionally, and bleed lines if necessary.

    Check electrical system functionally.

    Examine battery and top up to proper level with distilled water or diluted acid as may be required. Clean and tighten terminals.

    Inspect shock absorbers for leaks. Examine oil levels, and top up if necessary (piston type only).

    Test tyres for correct pressure.

    Check doors for ease in opening and closing. If necessary, lightly smear with a suitable lubricating agent all dovetails and striking plates.

    Where the Jackall jacking system is in use, check union nuts to recommended pressures, and if necessary top up the fluid reservoir.

ALL MATERIALS CHARGEABLE TO THE CUSTOMER

SPARKING PLUGS

Sparking Plug Gap
Replacing Sparking Plugs · Air Cleaner

SPARKING PLUGS

The sparking plugs are of great importance to satisfactory engine performance and the correct type should be used for replacement. There is little to be gained by experimenting with different plugs, as those fitted as standard equipment are best suited to the engine. These are Champion NA8, 14 mm., and the gap between the points should be from ·020 to ·022 in. (·5 to ·56 mm.).

When adjusting the gap always move the side wire—never bend the centre wire. The Champion Sparking Plug Co. supply a special combination gauge and setting tool which is recommended.

To save fuel and ensure easy starting the plugs should be cleaned and tested at intervals of 3,000 miles (5000 km.), preferably by a garage with a special air-blast service unit.

Plugs which are oily, dirty or corroded like the one shown on the right cannot give good results. Every 12,000 miles (20000 km.) it will be found economical to fit a set of new plugs.

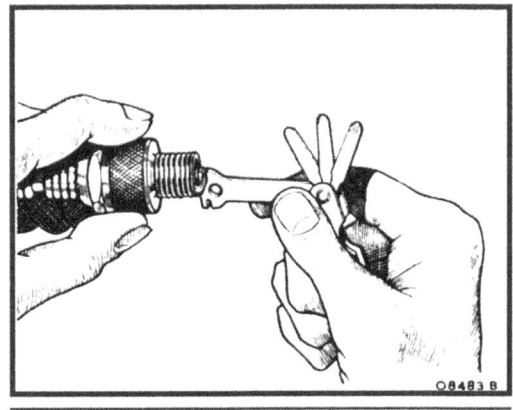

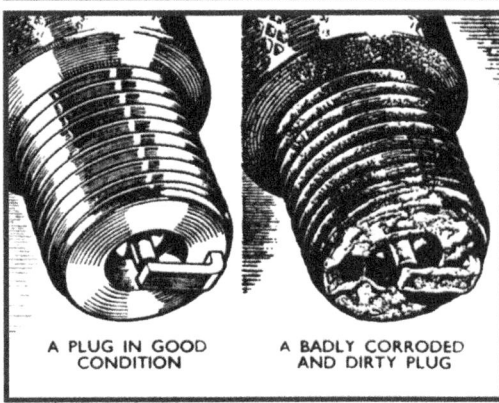

A PLUG IN GOOD CONDITION   A BADLY CORRODED AND DIRTY PLUG

AIR CLEANER (A)

Every 3,000 miles (5000 km.) wash the filter element in petrol (gasoline) and allow to dry. Re-oil the element with S.A.E. 20 engine oil and allow to drain before re-assembling.

When servicing, it is only necessary to withdraw the two hexagon-headed screws and lift off the outer cover to release the corrugated element. Reassemble the front element with the corrugations clear of the breather spigot in the main filter case.

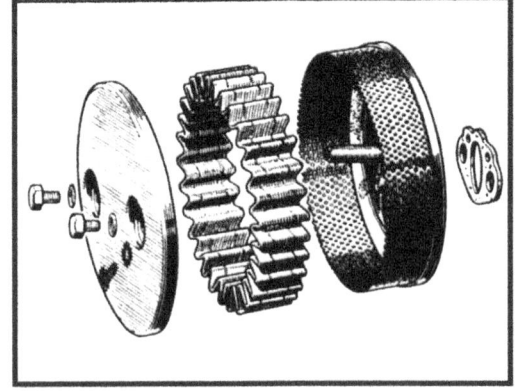

Cleaning the Filters · Adjusting the Slow Running · Adjusting Mixture Control Linkage

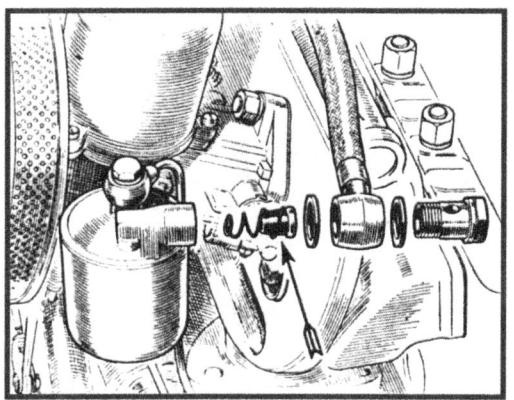

CARBURETTER FILTERS

To ensure a free flow of fuel to the float-chambers the filters should be removed at intervals of about 6,000 miles (10000 km.) and thoroughly cleaned with a stiff brush and fuel. Never use rag. The filters are situated behind the banjo-type union at the junction of the fuel pipe to each float-chamber lid.

Replace the filters with their helical springs first and their open ends outwards. Replace the fibre washers correctly.

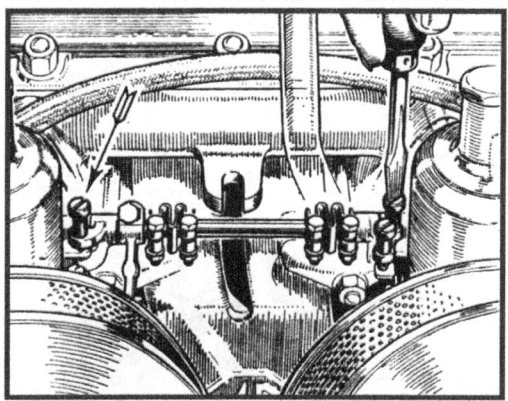

SLOW-RUNNING ADJUSTMENT

Slow-running adjustments are carried out by adjusting the position of the carburetter throttle lever stop screws, which are spring-loaded, until gentle slow running is attained.

It is important that both carburetters are set **exactly** alike and you are advised to entrust this to an M.G. Dealer.

Make sure that there is a small clearance between the mixture and throttle interconnecting lever and its abutment screw.

MIXTURE CONTROL LINKAGE ADJUSTMENT

When the mixture control knob on the instrument panel is right home there must be a small gap between the adjusting screw and the interconnecting lever on the front carburetter. This gap determines the degree of interlinkage between the throttle and the mixture control and should be set so that there is just clearance between the end of the adjusting screw and the anvil of the rocking lever linked to the jet operating lever.

CARBURETTERS
Adjusting the Jets

ADJUSTING THE JETS

Run the engine until it attains its normal running temperature. Set the slow-running screws on the carburetter throttle actuating levers so that the throttles are both open the same amount. This is indicated by the same suction noise at each carburetter.

Disconnect the mixture control wire from the end of the brass lever actuating the jets, and screw the jet adjusting nuts well downwards. Note that the jet actuating levers must be kept in contact with the jet heads the whole time.

The jet adjusting nuts should now be unscrewed upwards slowly (thus gradually weakening the mixture) until the engine idles evenly, firing on all cylinders regularly, and running at its best speed. This will be the normal slow-running position when the engine is hot, and as the jet needles are of the correct size the general performance on the road should be entirely satisfactory. Check by raising each carburetter piston $\frac{1}{32}$ in. (·8 mm.) with the pin indicated by the arrow. It is not necessary to remove the air cleaner. If the engine speed increases momentarily the setting is right. If the engine stalls the setting is too weak. If the engine speed increases permanently it is too rich.

The mixture control wire may be reconnected when the adjustment is satisfactory, care being taken to see that the control knob has ample clearance when the jet is in contact with the adjusting nut. Final adjustment for slow running is then carried out by adjusting each of the carburetter throttle lever stop screws an equal amount.

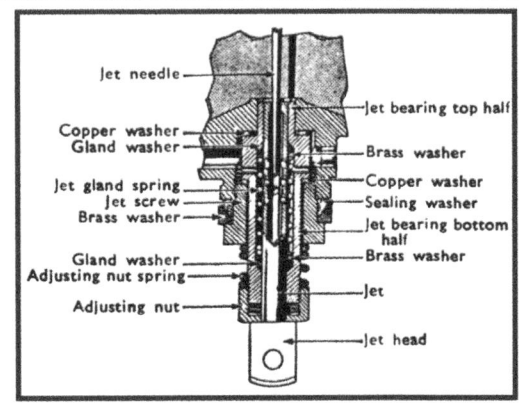

Jet needle
Jet bearing top half
Copper washer
Gland washer
Brass washer
Copper washer
Jet gland spring
Jet screw
Sealing washer
Brass washer
Jet bearing bottom half
Brass washer
Gland washer
Adjusting nut spring
Jet
Adjusting nut
Jet head

Cleaning the Fuel Pump Filter and Points Connections

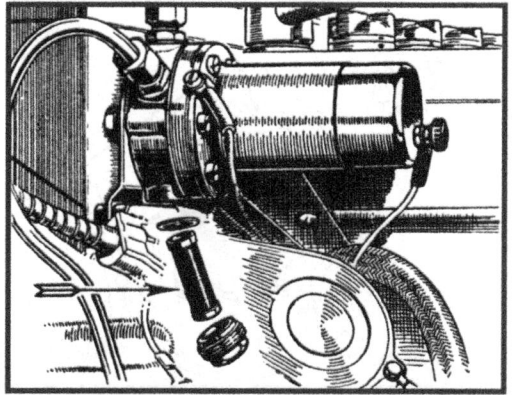

CLEANING THE FILTER

Every 6,000 miles (10000 km.) withdraw the fuel pump filter and clean it thoroughly in fuel. The filter is inserted into the bottom of the pump body and is easily withdrawn by unscrewing its hexagon attachment screw.

When cleaning it do not use rag; always use a stiff brush and clean fuel.

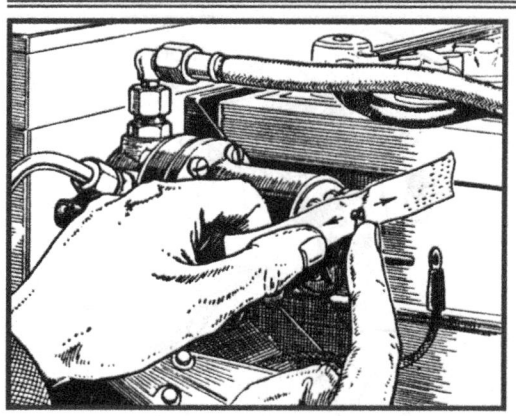

CLEANING THE CONTACT POINTS

The contact points can be cleaned by drawing a strip of clean note-paper between them while they are lightly held together.

If the points show signs of heavy pitting they should be entrusted to an M.G. Dealer for attention.

FUEL PUMP CONNECTIONS

The majority of pump troubles are caused by bad connections. Care must therefore be taken to ensure that all electrical connections to the pump are correctly made, particularly the earth wire at the terminal screw on the body and the main terminal on the bakelite end cover.

ELECTRICAL EQUIPMENT

Distributor Maintenance · Distributor, Cleaning Cover · Cleaning Contact Breaker

AFTER FIRST 500 MILES (800 Km.), THEN EVERY 3000 MILES (5000 Km.) Remove the distributor cap and turn the engine by hand until the contacts are fully opened. Check the gap with the gauge on the screwdriver supplied in the tool kit ; the gauge should be a sliding fit in the gap. If the gap varies appreciably from the gauge, slacken the two contact plate securing screws. Move the plate until the gap is correct and tighten the screws. The thickness of the gauge is ·016 in. (·41 mm.).

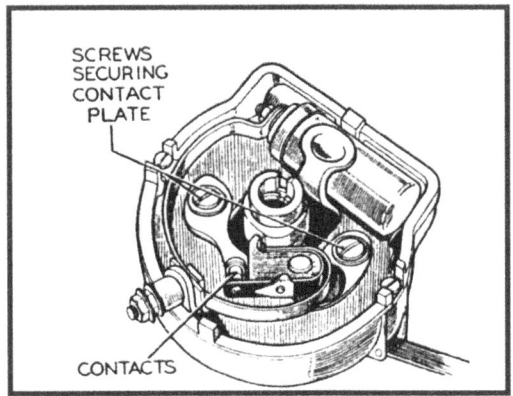

Distributor cleaning. Wipe the inside and outside of the moulded distributor cap with a soft dry cloth, paying particular attention to the space between the terminals. See that the small carbon brush on the moulding works freely in its holder.

If the contact breaker points are burned or blackened, clean them with a fine carborundum stone or with very fine emery-cloth. Afterwards wipe away any trace of dirt or metal dust with a petrol-moistened cloth.

Cleaning of the contacts is made easier if the contact breaker lever carrying the moving contact is removed. To do this unscrew the nut securing the end of the spring, remove the spring washer and flat washer and lift off the lever complete with spring. After cleaning, check the contact breaker setting on replacement.

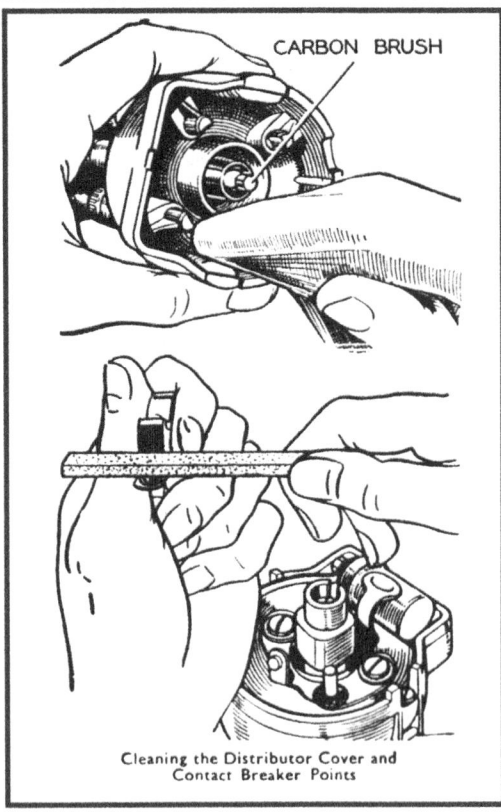

Cleaning the Distributor Cover and Contact Breaker Points

USE OF THE HYDROMETER

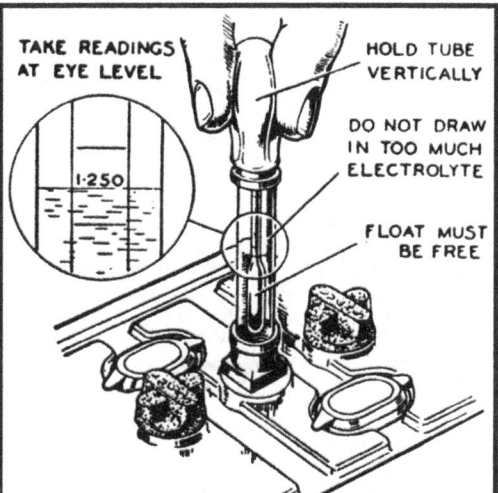

TAKE READINGS AT EYE LEVEL

1·250

HOLD TUBE VERTICALLY

DO NOT DRAW IN TOO MUCH ELECTROLYTE

FLOAT MUST BE FREE

Never leave the battery in a discharged condition for any length of time. Have it fully charged, and every fortnight give it a short refreshing charge to prevent any tendency for the plates to become permanently sulphated.

It is necessary to withdraw the plastic self-levelling device from the cell to allow use of the hydrometer on batteries fitted with the correct level device.

CHECKING SPECIFIC GRAVITY

Check the condition of the battery monthly or every 1,000 miles (1600 km.) by taking hydrometer readings of the specific gravity of the electrolyte in each of the cells. Readings should not be taken immediately after topping up the cells. The specific gravity readings and their indications are as follow:

1·280 to 1·300   Battery fully charged.

About 1·210   Battery about half-discharged.

Below 1·150   Battery fully dis-charged.

These figures are given assuming that the temperature of the solution is about 60° F. (16° C.). The readings for all cells should be approximately the same. If one cell gives a reading very different from the rest, it may be that acid has been spilled or has leaked from this particular cell, or there may be a short circuit between the plates, in which case the battery should be examined by a Lucas Service Depot or Agent.

ELECTRICAL EQUIPMENT
Dynamo Brushes
Starter Brushes · Dynamo Driving Belt

EVERY 12,000 MILES (20000 Km.)
Dynamo and starter brushes and commutator. Check that the brushes move freely in their holders by holding back the brush springs and pulling gently on the flexible connectors. If a brush is inclined to stick, remove it from its holder and clean its sides and the inside of the holder with a petrol-moistened rag. Replace the brushes in their original positions so as to maintain the correct 'bedding'. If the commutator is dirty, clean it by pressing a fine dry duster against it while the armature is slowly rotated. In the case of the dynamo this can be done by turning the engine over by hand, while with the starter the armature can be rotated by a spanner engaged on the square shaft extension at the commutator end after removing the protecting cap.

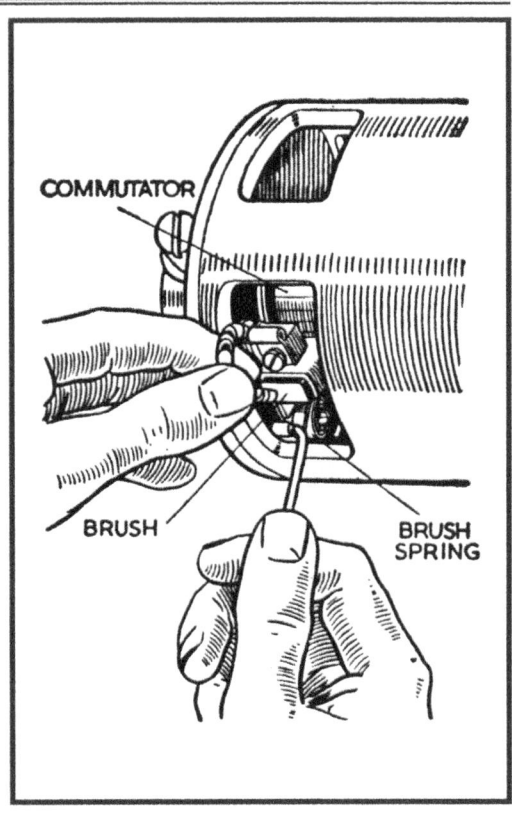

DYNAMO DRIVING BELT
Inspect the dynamo driving belt and adjust if necessary to take up any slackness. Care should be taken to avoid overtightening the belt, otherwise undue strain will be thrown on the dynamo bearings.
The belt tension is adjusted by slackening the bolts of the dynamo cradle and moving the dynamo the required amount by hand. Tighten up the three bolts thoroughly.

ELECTRICAL EQUIPMENT
Jammed Starter Pinion · Distributor
Electric Horns

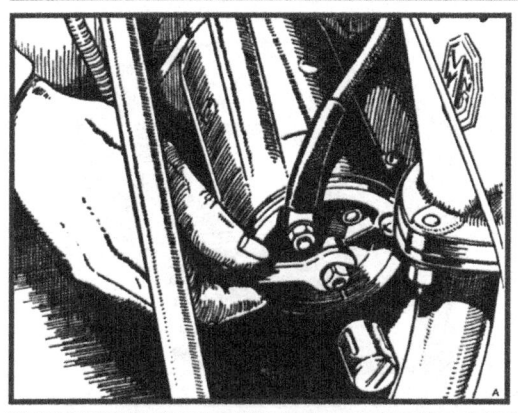

JAMMED STARTER PINION
In the event of the starter pinion becoming jammed in mesh with the flywheel, it can usually be freed by turning the starter armature by means of a spanner applied to the square end of the shaft extension at the commutator end, after removing the protecting cap.

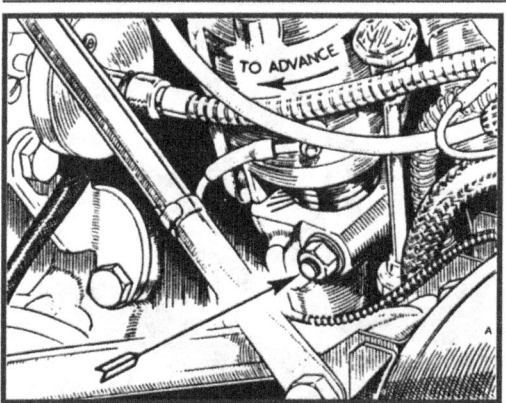

DISTRIBUTOR
The distributor is locked by the cotter bolt shown. If it is required to reset the firing point the position of the distributor body in relation to the housing should be marked, the cotter bolt nut loosened and the bolt tapped gently to release the distributor, which can then be rotated in the appropriate direction to give the desired result. The body should never be moved more than $\frac{1}{32}$ in. (·8 mm.) at a time and the cotter bolt must always be retightened before turning engine.

ELECTRIC HORNS
All horns, before being passed out of the Works, are adjusted to give their best performance, and will give a long period of service without any attention ; no adjustment should be required for a long period. There is no provision for altering the ' note ' of the horns.

ELECTRICAL EQUIPMENT
Control Box
Fuses · Spare Fuses

CONTROL BOX
The cut-out and regulator are accurately set before leaving the Works and they must not be tampered with. The cover protecting them is therefore sealed. The fuses are carried in a separate fusebox and are accessible without removing the cover protecting the regulator and cut-out units.

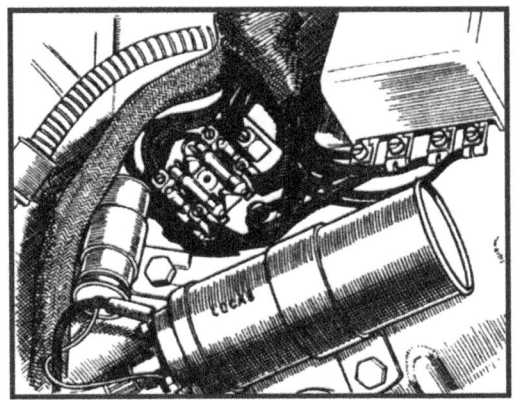

FUSES
Fuse connecting 'A1' and 'A2'.
This fuse protects the accessories which are connected so that they operate irrespective of whether the ignition is on or off.

Fuse connecting 'A3' and 'A4'.
This fuse protects the accessories which are connected so that they operate only when the ignition is switched on. (Stop lamps, etc.)

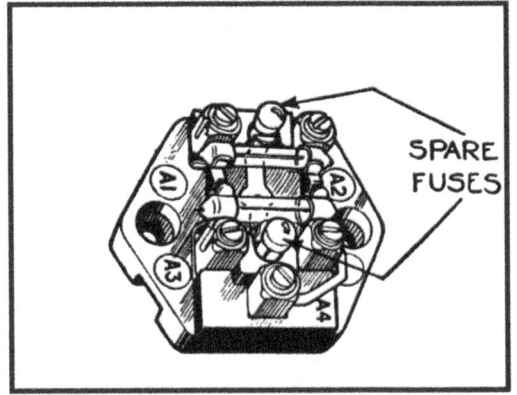

SPARE FUSES

SPARE FUSES
Spare fuses are provided and it is important to use only the correct replacement fuse. The fusing value is marked on a coloured paper slip inside the glass tube of the fuse. If the new fuse blows immediately and the cause of the trouble cannot be found, have the equipment examined at a Lucas Service Depot.

ELECTRICAL EQUIPMENT
Blown Fuses · Renewing High-tension Cables
Direction Indicator Unit

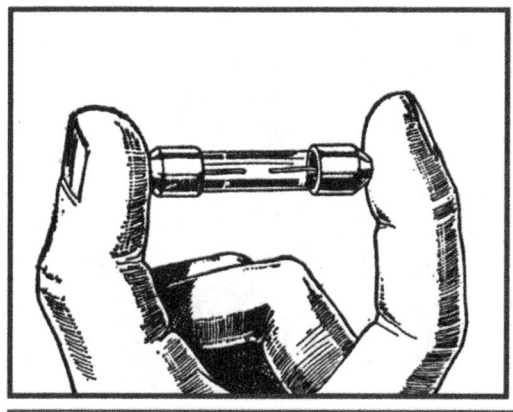

BLOWN FUSES

The units which are protected by the fuses can readily be identified on the wiring diagram. A blown fuse is indicated by the failure of all the units protected by it, and is confirmed by examination of the fuse when withdrawn. Before replacing a blown fuse, inspect the wiring of the units that have failed for evidence of a short circuit, or other fault. Remedy the cause of the trouble before fitting a new fuse.

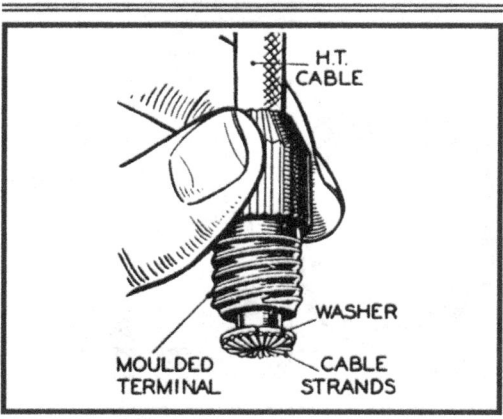

H.T. CABLE

WASHER

MOULDED TERMINAL   CABLE STRANDS

RENEWING HIGH-TENSION CABLES

The high-tension cables connecting the coil to the distributor and the distributor to the sparking plugs may, after long use, show signs of perishing. They must then be replaced by 7 mm. rubber-covered ignition cable.

Bare the end of the cable for ¼ in., pass it through its moulded terminal and washer and spread out the strands to ensure good contact. Occasionally check that the terminal connections are quite tight.

DIRECTION INDICATOR UNIT

The flasher unit is attached to the tool box near the voltage control box. It is non-adjustable and does not require any maintenance. The relay unit on the engine bulkhead below the flasher is sealed also and is non-adjustable.

ELECTRICAL EQUIPMENT
Removing and Replacing Light Unit
Replacing Bulbs

REMOVING THE LIGHT UNIT

To remove the light unit for bulb replacement, unscrew the securing screw at the bottom of the lamp rim and lift off the rim. Remove the dust-excluding rubber, which will reveal three spring-loaded screws. Press the light unit inwards against the tension of the springs and turn it in an anti-clockwise direction until the heads of the screws can pass through the enlarged ends of the keyhole slots in the rim.

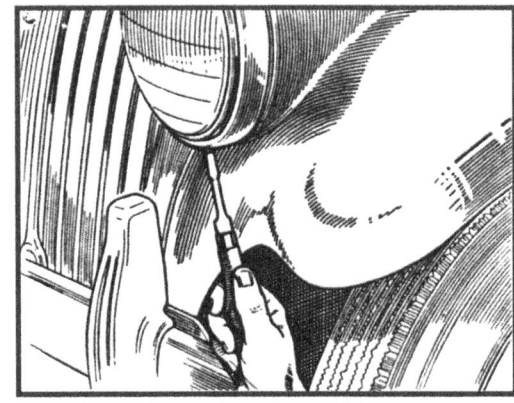

REPLACING BULBS

Withdrawal of the light unit gives immediate access to the bulb carrier for replacement. Twist the back-shell anti-clockwise and pull it off. The bulb can then be withdrawn from its holder.

Fit the replacement bulb in the holder, with the slot in its disc in engagement with the projection in the holder. Engage the projections on the back-shell with the holder slots, press on and twist to the right until its catch engages.

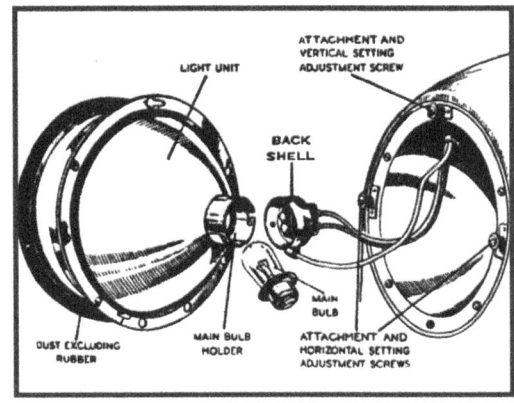

REPLACING BULBS

Withdrawal of the light unit gives immediate access to the bulb carrier for replacement. Twist the back-shell anti-clockwise and pull it off. The bulb can then be withdrawn from its holder.

Fit the replacement bulb in the holder, with the slot in its disc in engagement with the projection in the holder. Engage the projections on the back-shell with the holder slots, press on and twist to the right until its catch engages.

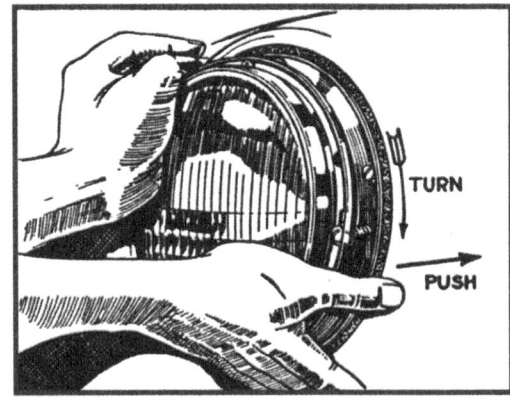

ELECTRICAL EQUIPMENT

Setting Headlamps · Sidelamps
Number-plate Lamp

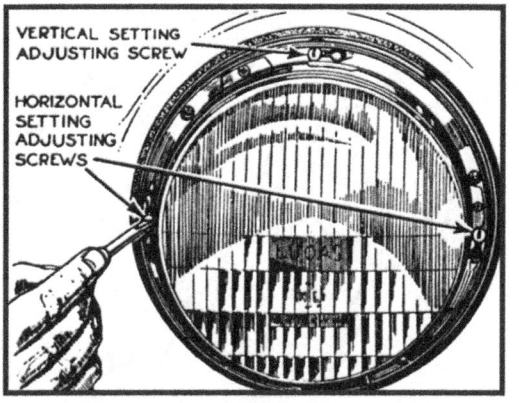

VERTICAL SETTING ADJUSTING SCREW

HORIZONTAL SETTING ADJUSTING SCREWS

SETTING HEADLAMPS

The lamps should be set so that the main driving beams are parallel with the road surface or in accordance with local regulations. If adjustment is required, remove the rim as described on page 54. Vertical adjustment is made by turning the screw at the top of the lamp. Horizontal adjustment can be altered by using the adjustment screws on each side of the light unit.

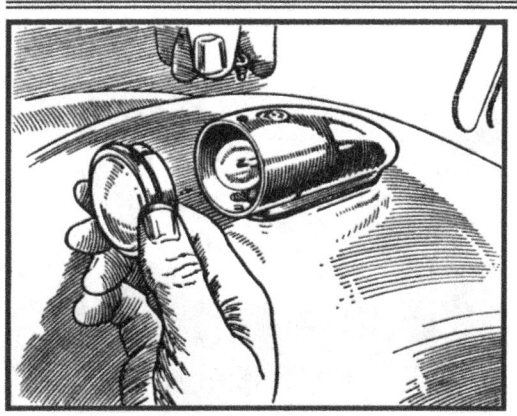

SIDELAMPS

To reach the bulb in a sidelamp, take out the screw in the top of the lamp and withdraw the glass and rim forward.
The bulb has a bayonet fitting.

NUMBER-PLATE LAMP

A single bayonet-fixing bulb is fitted and the cover may be removed after slackening the small retaining screw.

ELECTRICAL EQUIPMENT
Tail Lamp Bulb Replacement
Panel Lights • Replacement Bulbs

TAIL LAMP BULB REPLACEMENT

The rim and glass of the combined tail lamps and stop lamps are held in the grooves of the rubber housing and may be removed and replaced with the fingers only.

The dual-filament bulbs must be replaced the right way round to provide the brighter light for stop indication. To facilitate this the bulbs are of a special type which cannot be fitted incorrectly.

When replacing the lamp rim it should be engaged at the top first.

PANEL AND MAP LIGHTS

There are three lamps illuminating the instruments and their locations are shown in the accompanying illustration.

To obtain access to them it is necessary to remove the protective panel under the fascia board. There is one in each of the casings for the revolution indicator and speedometer, and one above the ammeter.

The map lamp above each glovebox may be withdrawn from its bracket to facilitate bulb renewal.

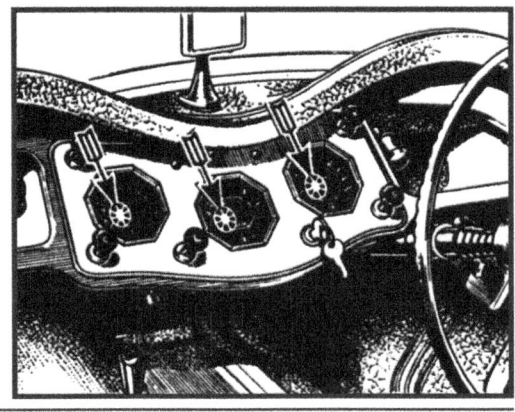

REPLACEMENT BULBS (12-VOLT)

	Watts		B.M.C. Part No.
Headlamps, Home and Export (RHD) (dip left)	42/36	(pre-focus)	3H1892
Headlamps, Export and U.S.A. (LHD) (dip right)	42/36	(pre-focus)	3H1893
Headlamps Export (Europe, except France) ...	45/40	(pre-focus)	3H921
Sidelamp	6/21	(S.C.C.) ...	1F1026
Stop/tail lamp (irreversible)	6/21	(S.B.C.) ...	1F1026
Number-plate lamp	6	(M.C.C.)...	2H4817
Panel lights and main beam warning light ...	2·2	(M.E.S.) ...	2H4732
Ignition warning light	2·2	(M.E.S.) ...	2H4732
Fuel warning light	2·2	(M.E.S.) ...	2H4732
Flasher warning light	2·2	(M.E.S.) ...	2H4732
Map-reading lights	2·2	(M.E.S.) ...	2H4732
Flashing direction indicators	21	(S.B.C.) ...	1G9012

The headlamp beam setting should be checked, and reset if necessary, every 12,000 miles (20000 km.) or at least once a year.

Checking and adjustment (see pages 54-5) may well be undertaken when the thinner engine oil and anti-freeze are introduced in preparation for winter service. This work should be entrusted to a Dealer or Distributor equipped with beam-testing apparatus.

IMPORTANT

Your attention is drawn to the following points, compliance with which, we suggest, will prove mutually beneficial.

I. WARRANTY CERTIFICATE

(a) Completion of the Warranty Certificate 'tear-off slip' at the time of vehicle purchase when sent to the Factory will ensure registration of ownership by the British Motor Corporation.

(b) Retention of the Owner's portion of the Certificate, signed by the Distributor and Owner, in a safe place **in the vehicle** (by quickly establishing ownership) will help to expedite any adjustments under Warranty if such adjustments are required to be carried out by a B.M.C. Distributor and Dealer other than the supplier of your vehicle.

2. CLAIMS UNDER WARRANTY

Claims for the replacement of material or parts under Warranty must always be submitted to the supplying Distributor or Dealer, or, when this is not possible, to the nearest Distributor or Dealer, informing them of the Vendor's name and address.

3. PREVENTIVE MAINTENANCE

Service vouchers are produced for your convenience, and the use of these is the best safeguard against the possibility of abnormal repair bills at a later date.

Prevent rather than **Cure.**

4. REPLACEMENT PARTS

When Service Parts are required insist on genuine B.M.C. (MOWOG) Parts as these are designed and tested for your vehicle and in addition warranted for 12 months by the British Motor Corporation. ONLY WHEN GENUINE PARTS ARE USED CAN B.M.C. ACCEPT RESPONSIBILITY.

When purchasing replacement parts or having repairs done owners are requested to see that a label similar to the one illustrated here is attached to the invoice rendered. These labels are issued by B.M.C. Service Limited for the Home Trade and by Nuffield Exports Limited for the Overseas Trade and they constitute a guarantee that genuine B.M.C. parts are supplied.

Our worldwide network of Distributors and Dealers is at your service.

INDEX

INDEX

M.G. MIDGET (Series TF and TF 1500)
LUBRICATION CHART

EVERY 250 MILES (400 Km.)

(1) ENGINE. Check the oil level with the dipstick, and top up if necessary with oil to Ref. A.

EVERY 500 MILES (800 Km.)

(2) STEERING JOINT NIPPLES. Give three or four strokes of the grease gun filled with oil to Ref. D.

AFTER THE FIRST 500 MILES (800 Km.)

(3) ENGINE. Drain off the old oil and refill with fresh oil to Ref. A.

(4) GEARBOX. Drain off the old oil and refill with fresh oil to Ref. B.

(5) REAR AXLE. Drain off the old oil and refill with fresh oil to Ref. B.

EVERY 1,000 MILES (1600 Km.)

(6) GEARBOX. Inspect the oil level with the dipstick, and top up as necessary with oil to Ref. B.

(7) REAR AXLE. Inspect the oil level through the filler, and top up as necessary with oil to Ref. B.

(8) PROPELLER SHAFT NIPPLES. Give three or four strokes of the grease gun filled with grease to Ref. D.

(9) CARBURETTERS. Remove the brass caps from the tops of the suction chambers and add a teaspoonful of engine oil to Ref. F.

(10) WATER PUMP. Give two strokes of the grease gun filled with grease to Ref. C.

(11) MASTER CYLINDER. Inspect the fluid level and top up with Lockheed Genuine Brake Fluid. DOOR LOCKS, CONTROL JOINTS, ETC. Lubricate with oil to Ref. F.

EVERY 3,000 MILES (5000 Km.)

(12) ENGINE. Drain off the old oil and refill with oil to Ref. A.

(13) DISTRIBUTOR. Withdraw the rotor and add a few drops of thin oil to Ref. F to the advance mechanism through the gap around the cam spindle and to the spindle through the cam securing screw duct. Smear the cam and the contact breaker pivot lightly with grease to Ref. D.

(14) DYNAMO. Remove the grease cap and refill with grease to Ref. C. AIR CLEANER. Clean and re-oil.

EVERY 6,000 MILES (10000 Km.)

(15) EXTERNAL OIL FILTER. Fit a new filter (throw-away type). Fit a new filter element (renewable-element type).

(16) GEARBOX. Drain off the old oil and refill with oil to Ref. B.

(17) REAR AXLE. Drain off the old oil and refill with oil to Ref. B.

(18) FRONT WHEEL BEARINGS. Remove the hub and grease caps and fill the caps with grease to Ref. C. REVOLUTION INDICATOR GEARBOX. Give two strokes of the grease gun with grease to Ref. B.

EVERY 12,000 MILES (20000 Km.)

(19) HYDRAULIC DAMPERS. Remove, clean, and inspect the fluid level. Top up with the recommended fluid.

(20) STEERING RACK. Give up to 10 strokes (not more) of the grease gun filled with oil to Ref. B to the nipple on the steering rack.

MULTIGRADE MOTOR OILS

In addition to the recommended lubricants listed in the Manual we approve the use of these new motor oils, as produced by the oil companies shown in our Manuals, for all climatic temperatures unless the engine is old and in poor mechanical condition. Some are more expensive than the recommended motor oils because of their special properties and greater fluidity at low temperatures.

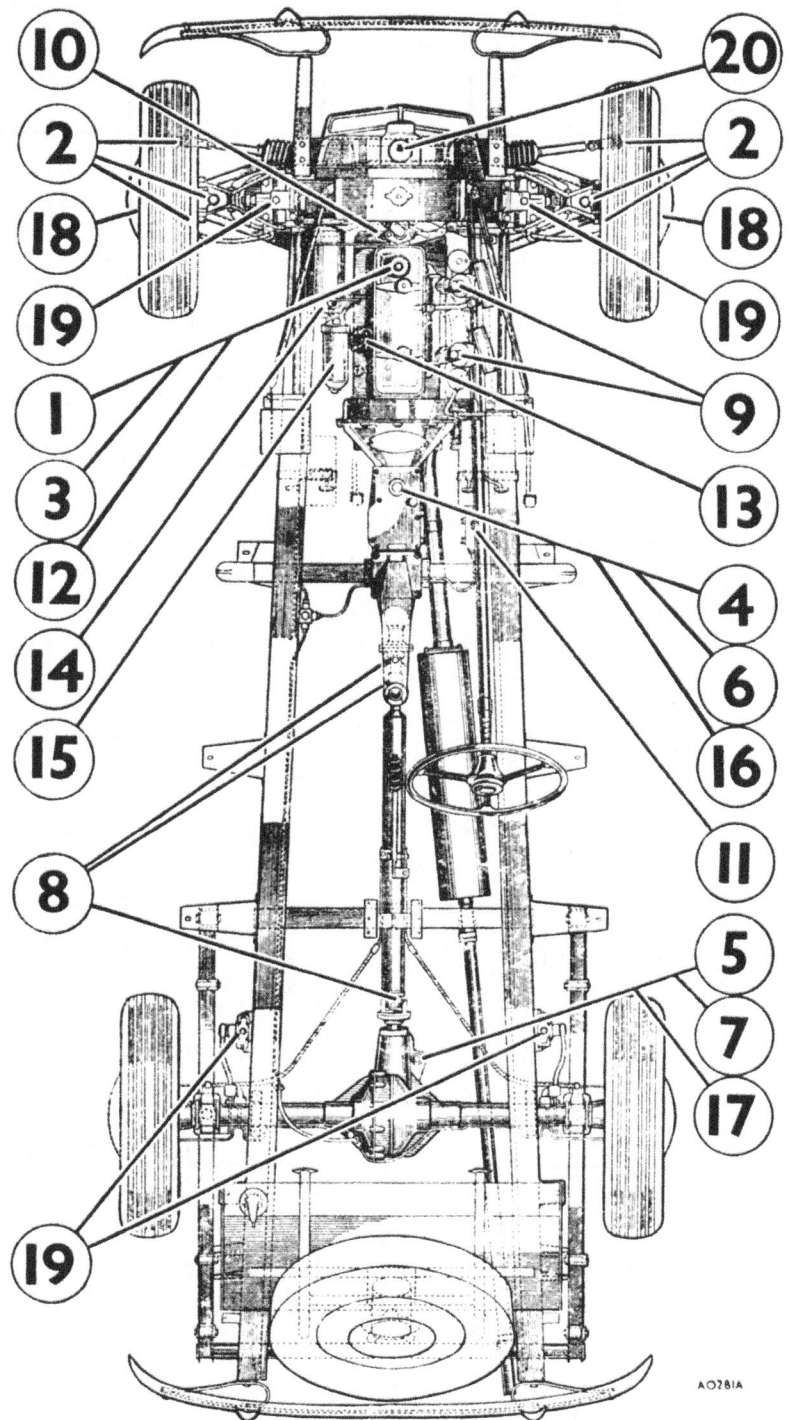

KEY TO RECOMMENDED LUBRICANTS

Component	A Engine and Air Cleaner			B Gearbox, Steering Gearbox and Rear Axle (Hypoid Gears)		C Wheel Hubs and Fan Bearings	D Chassis Greasing Nipples, etc.	E Cables and Control Joints	F Oilcan
Climatic conditions	Tropical and temperate down to 32° F. (0° C.)	Extreme cold down to 10° F. (−12° C.)	Arctic consistently below 10° F. (−12° C.)	All conditions down to 10° F. (−12° C.)	Arctic consistently below 10° F. (−12° C.)	All conditions	All conditions	All conditions	All conditions
SHELL	Shell X—100 30	Shell X—100 20/20W	Shell X—100 10W	Shell Spirax 90 E.P.	Shell Spirax 80 E.P.	Shell Retinax A	Shell Retinax A	Shell Retinax A	Shell X—100 20/20W
FILTRATE	Medium Filtrate 30	Zero Filtrate 20	Sub-Zero Filtrate 10W	Hypoid Filtrate Gear 90	Hypoid Filtrate Gear 80	Super Lithium Filtrate Grease	Super Lithium Filtrate Grease	Super Lithium Filtrate Grease	Zero Filtrate 20
STERNOL	Sternol W.W. 30	Sternol W.W. 20	Sternol W.W. 10	Ambroleum E.P. 90	Ambroleum E.P. 80	Ambroline L.H.T.	Ambroline L.H.T.	Ambroline L.H.T.	Sternol W.W. 20
DUCKHAM'S	Duckham's NOL Thirty	Duckham's NOL Twenty	Duckham's NOL Ten	Duckham's Hypoid 90	Duckham's Hypoid 80	Duckham's L.B. 10 Grease	Duckham's L.B. 10 Grease	Duckham's L.B. 10 Grease	Duckham's NOL Twenty
CASTROL	Castrol X.L.	Castrolite	Castrol Z	Castrol Hypoy	Castrol Hypoy Light	Castrolease L.M.	Castrolease L.M.	Castrolease L.M.	Castrolite
ESSO	Esso Extra Motor Oil 20W/30	Esso Extra Motor Oil 20W/30	Essolube Motor Oil 10	Esso Expee Compound 90	Esso Expee Compound 80	Esso Multi-purpose Grease H	Esso Multi-purpose Grease H	Esso Multi-purpose Grease H	Essolube Extra Motor Oil 20W/30
MOBIL	Mobiloil A	Mobiloil Arctic	Mobiloil 10W	Mobilube G.X. 90	Mobilube G.X. 80	Mobilgrease M.P.	Mobilgrease M.P.	Mobilgrease M.P.	Mobiloil Arctic
BP ENERGOL	Energol S.A.E. 30	Energol S.A.E. 20W	Energol S.A.E. 10W	Energol E.P. S.A.E. 90	Energol E.P. S.A.E. 80	Energrease L.3	Energrease L.3	Energrease L.3	Energol S.A.E. 20W

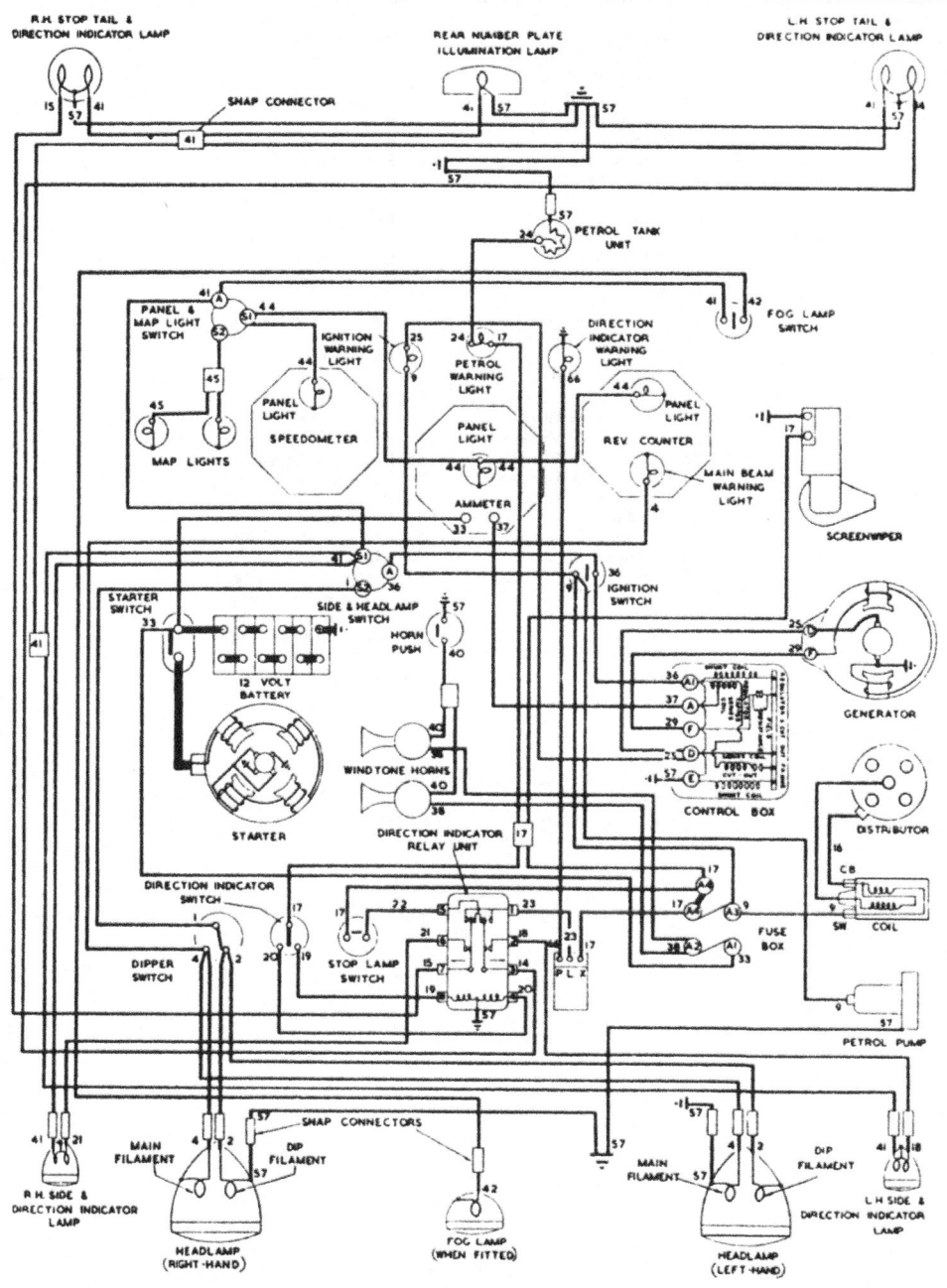

WIRING DIAGRAM
Home and Export (Right- and Left-hand Drive)

KEY TO CABLE COLOURS

1	Blue	34	Brown *with* Red
2	Blue *with* Red	35	Brown *with* Yellow
3	Blue *with* Yellow	36	Brown *with* Blue
4	Blue *with* White	37	Brown *with* White
5	Blue *with* Green	38	Brown *with* Green
6	Blue *with* Purple	39	Brown *with* Purple
7	Blue *with* Brown	40	Brown *with* Black
8	Blue *with* Black	41	Red
9	White	42	Red *with* Yellow
10	White *with* Red	43	Red *with* Blue
11	White *with* Yellow	44	Red *with* White
12	White *with* Blue	45	Red *with* Green
13	White *with* Green	46	Red *with* Purple
14	White *with* Purple	47	Red *with* Brown
15	White *with* Brown	48	Red *with* Black
16	White *with* Black	49	Purple
17	Green	50	Purple *with* Red
18	Green *with* Red	51	Purple *with* Yellow
19	Green *with* Yellow	52	Purple *with* Blue
20	Green *with* Blue	53	Purple *with* White
21	Green *with* White	54	Purple *with* Green
22	Green *with* Purple	55	Purple *with* Brown
23	Green *with* Brown	56	Purple *with* Black
24	Green *with* Black	57	Black
25	Yellow	58	Black *with* Red
26	Yellow *with* Red	59	Black *with* Yellow
27	Yellow *with* Blue	60	Black *with* Blue
28	Yellow *with* White	61	Black *with* White
29	Yellow *with* Green	62	Black *with* Green
30	Yellow *with* Purple	63	Black *with* Purple
31	Yellow *with* Brown	64	Black *with* Brown
32	Yellow *with* Black	65	Dark Green
33	Brown	66	Light Green

OFFICIAL TECHNICAL BOOKS

Brooklands Technical Books has been formed to supply owners, restorers and professional repairers with official factory literature.

Workshop Manuals

Midget Instruction Manual		9781855200739
Midget TD & TF	AKD580A	9781870642552
MGA 1500 1600 & 1600 Mk. 2	AKD600D	9781869826307
MGA Twin Cam	AKD926B	9781855208179
Austin-Healey Sprite Mk. 2, Mk. 3 & Mk. 4 and		
MG Midget Mk. 1, Mk. 2 & Mk. 3		
	AKD4021	9781855202818
Midget 1500	AKM4071B	9781855201699
MGB & MGB GT	AKD3259 & AKD4957	9781855201743
MGB GT V8 Supplement		9781855201859
MGB, MGB GT and MGB GT V8		9781783180578
MGC	AKD 7133	9781855201828
Rover 25 & MG ZR 1999-2005		
	RCL0534ENGBB	9781855208834
Rover 75 & MG ZT 1999-2005		
	RCL0536ENGBB	9781855208841
MGF - 1.6 MPi, 1.8 MPi, 1.8VVC		
RCL 0051ENG, RCL0057ENG		
& RCL0124		9781855207165
MGF Electrical Manual 1996-2000 MY		
	RCL0341	9781855209077
MG TF	RCL0493	9781855207493

Parts Catalogues

MGA 1500	AKD1055	9781870642569
MGA 1600 Mk. 1 & Mk. 2	AKD1215	9781870642613
Austin-Healey Sprite Mk. 1 & Mk. 2 and		
MG Midget Mk. 1 (Mechanical & Body Edition)		
AKD3566 & AKD3567		9781783180509
Austin-Healey Sprite Mk. 3 & Mk. 4 and		
MG Midget Mk. 2 & Mk. 3 (Mechanical & Body		
Edition 1969)	AKD3513 & AKD3514	9781783180554
Austin-Healey Sprite Mk. 3 & Mk. 4 and		
MG Midget Mk. 2 & Mk. 3 (Feb 1977 Edition)		
	AKM0036	9780948207419
MGB up to Sept 1976	AKM0039	9780948207068
MGB Sept 1976 on	AKM0037	9780948207440

Owners Handbooks

Midget Series TD		9781870642910
Midget TF and TF 1500		
Operation Manual	AKD658A	9781870642934
MGA 1500	AKD598G	9781855202924
MGA 1600	AKD1172C	9781855201668
MGA 1600 Mk. 2	AKD1958A	9781855201675
MGA Twin Cam (Operation)	AKD879	9781855207929
MGA Twin Cam (Operation)	AKD879B	9781855207936
MGA 1500 Special Tuning	AKD819A	9781783181728
MGA 1500 and 1600 Mk. 1 Special Tuning		
	AKD819B	9781783181735
Midget TF and TF 1500	AKD210A	9781855202979
Midget Mk. 3 (GB 1967-74)	AKD7596	9781855201477
Midget (Pub 1978)	AKM3229	9781855200906
Midget Mk. 3 (US 1967-74)	AKD7883	9781855206311
Midget Mk. 3 (US 1976)	AKM3436	9781855201767
Midget Mk. 3 (US 1979)	AKM4386	9781855201774
MGB Tourer (Pub 1965)	AKD3900C	9781869826741

MGB Tourer & GT (Pub 1969)	AKD3900J	9781855200609
MGB Tourer & GT (Pub 1974)	AKD7598	9781869826727
MGB Tourer & GT (Pub 1976)	AKM3661	9781869826703
MGB GT V8	AKD8423	9781869826710
MGB Tourer & GT (US 1968)	AKD7059B	9781870642514
MGB Tourer & GT (US 1971)	AKD7881	9781870642521
MGB Tourer & GT (US 1973)	AKD8155	9781870642538
MGB Tourer (US 1975)	AKD3286	9781870642545
MGB (US 1979)	AKM8098	9781855200722
MGB Tourer & GT Tuning	CAKD4034L	9780948207051
MGB Special Tuning 1800cc	AKD4034	9780948207006
MGC	AKD4887B	9781869826734
MGF (Modern shape)	RCL0332ENG	9781855208339

Owners Workshop Manuals - Autobooks

MGA & MGB & GT 1955-1968	
(Glove Box Autobooks Manual)	9781855200937
MGA & MGB & GT 1955-1968	
(Autobooks Manual)	9781783180356
Austin-Healey Sprite Mk. 1, 2, 3 & 4 and	
MG Midget Mk. 1, 2, 3 & 1500 1958-1980	
(Glove Box Autobooks Manual)	9781855201255
Austin-Healey Sprite Mk. 1, 2, 3 & 4 and	
MG Midget Mk. 1, 2, 3 & 1500 1958-1980	
(Autobooks Manual)	9781783180332
MGB & MGB GT 1968-1981	
(Glove Box Autobooks Manual)	9781855200944
MGB & MGB GT 1968-1981	
(Autobooks Manual)	9781783180325

Carburetters

SU Carburetters Tuning Tips & Techniques	
	9781855202559
Solex Carburetters Tuning Tips & Techniques	
	9781855209770
Weber Carburettors Tuning Tips and Techniques	
	9781855207592

Restoration Guide

MG T Series Restoration Guide	9781855202115
MGA Restoration Guide	9781855203020
Restoring Sprites & Midgets	9781855205987
Practical Classics On MGB Restoration	9780946489428

MG - Road Test Books

MG Gold Portfolio 1929-1939	9781855201941
MG TA & TC GOLD PORT 1936-1949	9781855203150
MG TD & TF Gold Portfolio 1949-1955	9781855203167
MG Y-Type & Magnette Road Test Portfolio	9781855208629
MGB & MGC GT V8 GP 1962-1980	9781855200715
MGA & Twin Cam Gold Portfolio 1955-1962	9781855200784
MGB Roadsters 1962-1980	9781869826109
MGC & MGB GT V8 LEX	9781855203631
MG Midget Road Test Portfolio 1961-1979	9781855208957
MGF & TF Performance Portfolio 1995-2005	9781855207073
Road & Track On MG Cars 1949-1961	9780946489398
Road & Track On MG Cars 1962-1980	9780946489817

From MG specialists, Amazon and all good motoring bookshops.
Brooklands Books Ltd., P.O. Box 904, Amersham, Bucks, HP6 9JA, England, UK

www.brooklandsbooks.com

Brooklands Books Ltd., PO Box 904,
Amersham, HP6 9JA, UK
brooklandsbooks.com

Part Number: AKD658A

ISBN 9781870642934   Ref: MG26HH   1W6/2100

Made in the USA
Monee, IL
07 July 2026

56552026R00039